THE BIG PICTURE

God's Plan for Everything

Alistair Matheson

"He set it all out before us in Christ, a long-range plan in which everything would be brought together and summed up in Him, everything in deepest heaven, everything on planet earth."

EPHESIANS 1:10 (THE MESSAGE)

CONTENTS

Title Page   1

Copyright   2

Epigraph   3

Endorsements   7

Acknowledgements   11

Foreword   13

Prologue   17

The Big Picture: God's Plan for Everything   21

1. The Power of Unity   23

2. The Source of Unity   31

Part I: All of Christ   45

3. Revealing God   46

4. Redeeming Mankind   54

5. Raising Disciples   67

Part II: All the Church   80

6. Running the Church   81

7. The Holy Spirit   102

8. The Body of Christ   119

9. Every Gift Supplied   134

Part III: All Creation   151

10. Kosmos   152

11. To the Ends of the Earth   164

12. To the End of the Age   173

Epilogue   195

Books By This Author   199

ENDORSEMENTS

Huge thanks to all these in-demand leaders whom I respect so much, for so willingly taking the time to view my manuscript and responded so generously. Together, I sincerely believe we are right now in the 'sweet spot' of Kingdom potential that has ever been there for any generation of leaders willing to put the Big Picture before 'their thing'.

The Big Picture is most inspiring, encouraging and filled with hope concerning God's eternal purpose in Christ Jesus. This book provides a great grounding and understanding, and a springboard for sending God's people forth with the good news of the kingdom of God in the power of His Spirit.

As I read I could almost hear Alistair preaching with such enthusiasm as he is captivated by the fullness of God's awesome plan of redemption for His cosmos. This book will expand your vision, lifting you out of any small-mindedness, and propelling you forward into your part in making all of Christ known to all creation.

Steven Anderson
Apostolic leader, mentor and author, Glasgow

I thoroughly enjoyed The Big Picture *and it is a timely word in this season, like someone pressing the reboot button as we discuss what 'church' should look like post-pandemic.*

So many have never been as 'connected' to the world as this generation are, through their devices, yet have been starved of the 'meta-narrative', the big picture that makes sense of everything.

I always think of being lost in a massive shopping centre and finding a map that tells you where your destination is, but we still remain lost until we can find the little arrow on the map that says "YOU ARE HERE!". This book is that invaluable arrow that says, "You are here"!

Phelim Doherty
Pastor, author and veterinary surgeon, Derry

Alistair gently draws you into an exploration of who Jesus truly is. It's a subtle apologetic that is easy to read and understand. If I was someone seeking to find out more about Christianity but hadn't yet committed this book would help me understand why I should commit to Christ, what steps I would need to take after I commit to Christ, and those with whom I would need to journey in order to grow as a Christian. I highly recommend this book.

Yinka Oyekan
President of the Baptist Union of Great Britain

The author's passion and insight are clearly revealed as he unfolds the wonder of God's plan in eternity being outworked in history. Of particular relevance today, in this new season, is the author's unpacking of the church's glorious destiny. This book has the hallmark of apostolic authenticity and authority on every page.

Ivan Parker
National Leader, Apostolic Church UK

The iconic slogan, It does what it says on the tin, *could be applied to this book. In traumatic times, it's easy to retreat into a small vision that focuses on me, mine and my self-determined interests, but this is when we most need a big picture of who God is, how He works and what He's doing.*

Alistair deals with some foundational theological concepts that, if understood and engaged with, carry the potential to change your outlook and attitude. In an age of information, where people write because they have an opinion about everything, this is like fresh air for the soul. There's nothing 'showy' about it. This is a biblically faithful exploration of God and His purposes, composed by a faithful minister writing about his primary passions: Jesus, His church and His world. If you're a seasoned believer, The Big Picture *will serve to refresh you; if you're a new believer, it will establish you; if you're an unbeliever, it will provoke you.*

I love this book and I love its author even more.

Dom Bird

Lead Pastor, Sunnyhill Church, Poole

Jesus sent us to the ends of the earth with the beautiful promise, 'and I will be with you always to the very end of the age.'

In The Big Picture *Alistair invites us to meditate on Jesus; to think biblically and theologically; to love generously and wholeheartedly; and to serve bravely and confidently. Not a whip-crack to get us moving, but a bright torchlight illumining the path of discipleship.*

Humble, prophetic, urgent, gracious, theologically articulate, joyfully accessible and full of practical holiness. Read it!

James Faddes

Church Leader, Bishopbriggs Community Church

Alistair Matheson is a force of nature with a passion and commitment that is infectious. He is the embodiment of this book: not simply as its author but as its lived-out example – 'All of Christ in All the Church to All Creation' is Alistair's life and ambition.

The Big Picture *is an encouraging treatise illuminating God's great design for the Church and the world: it will feed your faith, inspire you to good works and wow you to wonder and worship again and again.*

Craig Hopkins

Lead Pastor, Brackla Tabernacle, Bridgend

The Big Picture *is wonderfully Christ-centred and thoroughly grounded in scripture. The key themes of the book are nothing new but Alistair addresses them with genuine insight and frequently profound innovation.*

Christ's glory enabling the church's unity! ... The interdependence of the Trinity inspiring the oneness of the church! ... The all-of-Godness that is Christ! ... The relational depth of sonship! ... The mindblowing implications of Jesus being Head of His church! ... The potency and intimacy of the Person of the Holy Spirit! ... The IMAX-picture view of the redemption work of Christ across the whole of creation!

My experience of reading this book was that my soul was quite literally refreshed with every chapter; waves of truth, swells of hope and the flow of true life. I trust it will do the same for you.

Simon Taylor
Pastor, Oakwood Church, Taunton

This is a timely book.

It is said that you must look at the big things whilst doing the small things so that all the small things go in the direction of the big thing. This panoramic view of the purposes of God from Alistair helps us do just that. It adds hope to the journey, purpose for the present and clarity for the way ahead.

Andrew Owen
Founder, Destiny Ministries

A truly inspiring read, providing a comprehensive span of God's intentional design and purpose for His church. It offers brilliant insight and revelation.

Paul Howells
Apostolic leader, Stockton-on-Tees

ACKNOWLEDGEMENTS

I am especially grateful to Steven Anderson, Phelim Doherty and Peter Vincent for taking the time to read my manuscript, offer helpful feedback, rescue me from red faces and regrets, and even spot a whole bunch of typos! After reading Peter's generous foreword, I'm left thinking, *Oh Lord, please let it do justice to that!*

Special thanks to Dom Bird who not only read and endorsed the manuscript, but went the extra mile and supplied a very much improved cover design. Writers looking for a designer who's just 'got it' need look no further than www.heraldpresenting-you.com.

I asked a wide range of respected Christian leaders to provide endorsements. My thinking was that, if even a quarter of them found time to pen a few words, I should be fine. Lo and behold, these heroes nearly all said 'yes', some going beyond the scanning of sample chapters to read the entire manuscript. I'm quite blown away - these are busy people with big priorities.

Big thanks also to John Caldwell, Scotland's latest Christian writing and publishing phenomenon, for repeatedly pointing me in the right direction, and for his contagious enthusiasm to simply go for it!

As with my Lockdown 1 devotional, *40 Days: Treasures of Dark-*

ness, I am indebted to my fellow prisoners of house arrest, Barbara - the proof reader to whom I owe most - and my son, Kenneth, both of whom have so patiently accepted *What-Do-You-Think?* as their new middle names on occasions they've tried to sneak past me unnoticed. Enter into your rest! Well, 'til next time ...

Finally, I'd like to acknowledge the huge inspiration of my fellow church leaders in Glasgow who epitomise an emerging generation that longs for our world to see a 'full-sized' Jesus, an image expressed through something way bigger than all our small corners. In Jesus, *The Big Picture* is always ours, never mine.

FOREWORD

"**I**f a book is well written, I always find it too short," said Jane Austen. I understand. There have been several in my lifetime. This is one of those books. Alistair Matheson's writing activates a keen appetite for more.

I find it as much a privilege as it is a pleasure to welcome you on board a journey as you read. It will carry you to the breathtaking heights of biblical revelation. This will not be a casual glance as you pass by, but like standing atop the Alps, the book portrays an inspiring panoramic view of God's agenda, a biblical understanding of the eternal purpose of God, and how He outworks it through the church in our times. This book is the product of a keen mind, a seeking heart and many years of prayerful openness to God's unfolding revelation of Scripture.

The Big Picture is distinctly framed by Alistair by these three profound statements which help us to focus on the direction of travel:

> 1. *There's nothing you need to know about God, that can't be seen in Jesus.*
>
> 2. *There's nothing of Jesus that He has not transplanted into His church.*

3. *There's nothing in the cosmos ultimately beyond the reach of the church.*

These are summed up in this memorable phrase – *"All of Christ, in All the Church, to All Creation."*

It does seem that Alistair has been *'... re-digging the old wells ...'* to discover a fresh and contemporary version of what an earlier generation of apostolic fathers, who carried a similar DNA of big-picture revelation found for their generation. To read *The Big Picture* reminds me of the Men of Isaachar who *"understood the times, and knew what Israel (God's people) should do ..."*

Readers, who may or may not be church leaders, will deeply appreciate the value of the contemporary relevance for the 21st century church in this book. Particularly so, as it moves out of a prolonged physical lockdown due to Covid-19, with the finger of faith on the reset button.

I really appreciate the keen biblical lucidity as Alistair delivers unmissable reading on how the 21st Century church lives in one common dispensation with the 1st century church. He demonstrates clearly that the purity and power of the Holy Spirit, along with the five ascension ministries of Ephesians 4, have never ceased to be foundational and currently essential to the ongoing life, ministry and effectiveness of the local and global church.

Succession in ministry for a city-centre church with some fifty different nationalities in attendance was no easy task to solve. But no problem to God. With divine precision, I was awakened in the very early hours one morning. God spoke the name of a man I hardly knew, and knew even less of his circumstances, who would succeed me in Glasgow at retirement. Long story made short, a set of circumstances literally brought us together that same day – and the result – Alistair Matheson has proved undeniably to be God's man for this season, not only for the city centre of Glasgow, but nationally and internationally, and an authentic apostolic leader of leaders.

I have great pleasure in recommending this book to you, and have every confidence that it will be an inspiration to everyone who is receptive to embrace the heights, depths and reach of the biblical truth of God's big picture and the practical implications.

I pray that it will become a tool of the Holy Spirit to help us all to accomplish His purpose in these days ... "*...until we all come to the whole measure of the fullness of Christ.*"

Peter Vincent
Preceding Pastor, Glasgow City Church

PROLOGUE

On a clear, fresh morning in Lockdown 2021, as I pedalled along the now familiar canal-side route of my regular exercise escape from house arrest, my mind hovering between the birds and buds of spring and the limbo of not even thinking, the significance of the date suddenly dawned on me.

April 1st.

On this day in 1942, more than two decades before my birth, the SS Rio Blanco was torpedoed by a U-boat near the American seaboard of the North Atlantic. My grandfather, Chief Officer John MacCorquodale, was one of 19 fatalities and my mum, aged 13, was left fatherless along with her younger brother.

As I continued cycling, I recalled my mum, now passed away, telling me of how this tragedy brought about the arrival into the family home of her grandmother, Mary, to support her widowed daughter-in-law in running the home and raising the family. According to Mum, Granny Mary was a wonderful woman and the brightest shining light for Jesus she ever knew, mothering them all, widow and children alike, deeply grieved though she was herself by the loss of her firstborn at sea.

Mary came from a Tiree family that produced at least two Christian ministers, one of them apparently a renowned hymn writer, and my mother grew up singing Mary's redemption songs. A generation later, in my own early childhood of austere Psalmody, Mum would occasionally gather her own children around the piano after what was, for us, the penance of Sabbath mornings, to sing songs that offered the same hope, joy and life that Mum first learned from her own granny.

I pulled over my bike at the bank of the canal, biting my lips as tears welled up and, for the very first time in my 57 years, uttered the words, *"Lord, I'm so sorry it's taken me so long to say this, but I thank you for Mary MacCorquodale."*

My tears were a confluence of three emotions: first, *gratitude* for a brilliant light turned on in one of our family's darkest nights; second, *repentance* that it had taken me this long to express gratitude for someone to whom I owe so much; and third, *wonder* at what other enormously important yet obvious things I may have been missing all along.

I have similar feelings now as I prepare to press 'Publish'.

It's taken me much too long to write this book.

Like my canal-side prayer, the things I've written were neither complicated nor hard to say, yet so important to be said and, potentially, a catalyst for gratitude, repentance and wonder to anyone who gets the picture.

It's not hyperbole to say that in the vision of this book is the answer to everything for everyone.

The Big Picture, almost by definition, is not mine but God's. It's way bigger than I. It dwarfs the imaginations of the greatest thinkers and the strategies of the biggest churches. There is no vision worth having that does not fit somewhere into God's.

The Big Picture is God's vision.

Others may explain it more impressively and fully than I, but for me it's taken nearly 40 years to sum it up in one banner:

ALL of Christ in *ALL* the Church to *ALL* Creation!

There is nothing of God that is not in Jesus Christ, the One in whom the Scriptures say the fullness of the godhead dwells bodily.

There is nothing of Jesus - and therefore of God - that has not been invested in His body, the Church, and that is not revealed most clearly where that body comes together to express Him in unity.

There is no part of the *"all things"* of God's created order, visible or invisible, on Earth or beyond, that is outwith the reach of the church God has birthed and is still building today.

Your personal calling and your church's or movement's mission, will never come remotely close to achieving its potential, until you've pulled over to the side of life's path and become gripped by something infinitely bigger than any and all of us.

Indeed, it is then that the purpose for which we were each created will begin, as never before, to find its place in God's plan for everything.

Having outrageously packed the infinite into a ten-word banner, it is my prayer that these twelve chapters will at least begin to *un*pack a bigger picture that will cause everything to make greater sense for you; a master plan that will ignite in you some of the things God had in mind when, in eons past before the creation of the world, He planned you.

Alistair Matheson
12th April 2021

THE BIG PICTURE: GOD'S PLAN FOR EVERYTHING

All of Christ ... in all the Church ... to all Creation

1. THE POWER OF UNITY

*"The glory which You have given Me
I have given to them, that they may
be one, just as We are one; I in them
and You in Me, that they may be
perfected in unity, so that the world
may know that You sent Me, and loved
them, even as You have loved Me."*

John 17:22-23

John chapter 17 is devoted to Jesus' final prayer for His disciples before He left this world.

Entering into His own dead of night, Jesus might have been expected to be consumed by His own Great Trouble. But what we find Him praying in these verses, exploding out of His personal pain, is effectively a declaration of the divine plan He had spent three years on earth preparing to launch.

Now, just when everyone thought He was defeated, everything was finally in place for not just His death and bodily resurrection, but His ascension to heaven and the ignition of His new earthly body, the Church.

Jesus is praying that the glory of God revealed on earth through

Him will now be demonstrated by the disciples' collective em-bodiment of His mission to all mankind, through a movement we have come to know, simply, as the church.

What an incredible thought that the glory God the Father gave to Jesus, Jesus has also given to His church!

But what is that glory? It is nothing less than the weighty mani-festation of the awesome wonder of all that God is. And for see-ing, believing eyes, the glory of God had been revealed through Jesus would soon be demonstrated by His followers.

God's glory in Christ

Listen to how John, in this same Gospel account, speaks of God's glory in Jesus:

> *"In the beginning was the Word, and the Word was with God, and the Word was God. ... And the Word be-came flesh, and dwelt among us, and we saw His glory, glory as of the only begotten from the Father, full of grace and truth."* John 1:1, 14

God Himself became flesh and in the body of a man showed His glory. The Eternal One became an object of His own creation and, through the life and ministry of Jesus, demonstrated every-thing that anyone could wish to know about God.

The writer to the Hebrews introduces Jesus similarly:

> *"... [The Son] is the radiance of [God's] glory and the exact representation of His nature ..."* Hebrews 1:3a

Note that word 'glory' again. God, in His glory, is perfectly repre-sented and radiated on Planet Earth through the incarnation of Jesus Christ.

This is one of the great miracles that sets the Christian faith apart from every other religion in history: the God of all things is fully and perfectly displayed in the body of a man.

What an awesome truth: there is absolutely nothing that anyone could possibly wish to know about the nature of God that is not to be found in a man called Jesus. All that is God is in Jesus.

Jesus Himself simplified it to six words:

> *"I and the Father are one."* John 10:30

Amazed?

Well, here is something more astonishing yet:

> *"The glory which You have given Me I have given to them, that they may be one, just as We are one; I in them and You in Me, that they may be perfected in unity, so that the world may know that You sent Me ..."*
> John 17:22-23 (Emphasis mine)

The God who revealed Himself in Jesus is still revealing Himself in the church which is Jesus' body.

Christ's glory in the church

Clearly, this does not confer on God's people the status of gods. Unlike the *'Word made flesh'*, Christ Himself, His disciples are created beings, mortal children of Adam and not divine in essence. Yet, by His grace and power, we have been made what Peter calls *"partakers of the divine nature"* (II Peter 1:4).

This means that the glorious nature of God revealed through Jesus' earthly ministry was intended to be revealed through the representatives who would become known collectively as

Christ's body, the church.

In fact, Jesus said that His glory would be displayed even more dramatically on earth from His ascended seat than it was during His earthly walk:

> *"Truly, truly, I say to you, he who believes in Me, the works that I do, he will do also; and greater works than these he will do; because I go to the Father."* John 14:12 (Emphasis mine)

Jesus was saying that, after He ascended to the Father, God would be glorified by even greater works than those already seen - no longer by one physical Man, but by a new community generated through this Man.

There was a foretaste of this during Jesus' earthly ministry, as He sent out His disciples with the delegated power to heal, deliver and preach the gospel of His kingdom.

But Jesus gave two explicit reasons for imparting His glory to His disciples. The first of these was their unity.

That they may be one

> *"The glory which You have given Me I have given to them, that they may be one, just as We are one ..."* John 17:22

Jesus gave His glory that His disciples might be one; that, out of their communion with Him, the same unity that He had with the Father might infuse their relationships with one another.

I have often reflected on an early biblical account that reveals the staggering power of unity.

I'm thinking of the building of the Tower of Babel in Genesis chapter 11 where, even outside of God, there was clearly enormous potential in united collaboration. Such was the potency in the oneness of purpose of that ancient people, that God Himself decided to intervene ...

> *"The Lord said, 'Behold, they are one people, and they all have the same language. And this is what they began to do, and now nothing which they purpose to do will be impossible for them.'"* Genesis 11:6 (Emphasis mine)

Their unity apparently made them a rival even to the purposes of God. Because of their evil intent, God Himself came down, confused their language and scattered them so that they could no longer build.

Now travel from the diabolic unity of Babel to the divinely inspired unity of Pentecost, and see the remarkable contrast between what was stopped by God in Genesis and what was unstopped by the Holy Spirit in the Book of Acts; the kind of unity, with its effects, that Jesus Himself prayed for before His death.

On the the first Pentecost Sunday, God filled their unity with an outpouring of His glory ...

> *"These all with one mind were continually devoting themselves to prayer ... When the day of Pentecost had come, they were all together in one place. And suddenly there came from heaven a noise like a violent rushing wind, and it filled the whole house where they were sitting."* Acts 1:14a; 2:1-2

This time, instead of confusing their speech and scattering the people, God brought a dispersed people together and instantly removed their language barriers, as a united church declared the mighty deeds of God in the diverse tongues of those gathered.

So, God's glory was given, firstly, so that His people might be one, and secondly, with a bigger picture in mind - the vision already revealed in Jesus' prayer.

That the world may know

> *"... I in them and You in Me, that they may be perfected in unity, so that the world may know that You sent Me ..."* John 17:23 (Emphasis mine)

Just as Jesus gave His glory for unity's sake, so He prayed for our unity for the mission's sake: that the world may come to know God through Christ revealed in His people.

This is the same John who wrote:

> *"For God so loved the world, that He gave His only begotten Son, that whoever believes in Him shall not perish, but have eternal life."* John 3:16

The outcome of the church's unity in the Spirit is a revelation of Jesus Christ that the world will never see when God's people are divided.

The world has yet to see the fullness of the outpouring of God's glory that will result when all of God's people 'get it together' by getting together.

King David sang of it in the Psalms:

> *"Behold, how good and how pleasant it is for brothers to dwell together in unity! It is like the precious oil upon the head, coming down upon the beard, even Aaron's beard, coming down upon the edge of his robes. It is like the dew of Hermon coming down upon the mountains of Zion; for there the Lord commanded*

the blessing - life forever." Psalm 133:1-3

When God's people are united in Jesus Christ, they will not have to pray for an outpouring of salvation. Such blessing has already been commanded by God Himself, identified as an inevitable consequence of the right conditions.

This was in the mind of Jesus Himself when He prayed, *"May they be one, that the world may know that You sent Me."*

It was the same longing that caused Paul's heart to burn with the Master's plan:

> *"... Until we all attain to the unity of the faith, and of the knowledge of the Son of God, to a mature man, to the measure of the stature which belongs to the fulness of Christ ..."* Ephesians 4:13

It was what moved Paul to declare in the same chapter:

> *"There is one body and one Spirit, just as also you were called in one hope of your calling; one Lord, one faith, one baptism, one God and Father of all who is over all and through all and in all."* Ephesians 4:4-6

Like the assembling of tiny fragments in a grand mosaic, as a united body comes together, one Jesus is revealed, and all creation gets to see Him. Such should be a moment, like no other, when *"... the earth will be filled with the knowledge of the glory of the Lord, as the waters cover the sea."* Habakkuk 2:14

From David's city of 'glorious things' in Psalm 87, to Paul's revelation of 'one new man' in Ephesians chapter 2, to Jesus' prayer for the world He was about to die for in John chapter 17 ... the place of unity is a realm of unimaginable blessing.

Unity is at the very heart of God's master plan - *All of Christ in All the Church to All Creation* - and we cannot even begin to consider *The Big Picture* without grasping it.

But where does this unity come from?

2. THE SOURCE
OF UNITY

*"... That they may be one, just as We
are one; I in them and You in Me, that
they may be perfected in unity ..."*

John 17:22b-23a

J esus never spoke or acted independently from His Father, out
of His own exclusive source. By His own repeated declaration, everything He expressed and demonstrated flowed
out of His own union with God the Father.

The unity of the Trinity

The Trinity, or the Triune God - Father, Son and Holy Spirit - is
the eternal community of Three Persons of one essence or substance, known simply as God, from Whom and for Whom all
things were created.

Jesus' prayer makes it clear that the unity through which alone
our mission will succeed is to be patterned after the unbreakable, eternal communion that exists between Him and the
Father. The Trinity is the model and source of the church's unity.

In Jesus' life and ministry, as with all Bible revelation, the Trinity
is much more than a statement of belief: it is the source of world-

changing power.

Over the years, I have sometimes wearied of well-meaning Christians saying, 'Oh, I'm not into theology.' I understand what is usually meant by this, that Christians need to stop arguing about complex, non-essential matters of interpretation, nit-picking over the letter of the law. They say that because such a posture is so often at the expense of effective and compassionate ministry, more about defending ivory towers than extending Christ's kingdom.

I get it.

But the answer is not to throw the baby out with the bath water; and make no mistake, the revelation of Scripture is very much 'the baby'. Without biblical revelation, my knowledge of Jesus has no more foundation than the philosophy of the day or, at worst, my mood of the moment.

Whatever you call it - biblical theology, doctrinal truth or revelation knowledge - Jesus' prayers and teachings on the Trinity in John's Gospel were bursting with it! When He interceded that we might be one just as He and the Father are one, His fundamental premise was this: the church will never succeed in making God's redemption plan known to mankind without a dynamic understanding of the Trinity as our pattern for life.

The biblical fact of the Trinity - Three yet One - may be difficult to get our heads around, but God would not give us such a revelation if it were not essential. The implications of Jesus' prayer for our unity are life-transforming and world-changing. Just as the success of our mission depends upon our unity, so our unity is based upon the communion modelled by the Trinity.

It must be stressed that this is not about unity for unity's sake. Jesus was not asking for an at-all-costs unity of mankind. Neither was He praying for unity of religions.

As a follower of Jesus Christ, I cannot have spiritual unity with Jehovah's Witnesses, Mormons or other neo-Christian sects that deny the Trinity from which alone true, God-inspired unity is sourced. Sects such as these, by rejecting the divinity of God the Son and His co-equal communion with the Father (which they passionately do), and the personhood of the Holy Spirit (which they call a force), reject the most fundamental building block of unity.

Similarly, world religions such as Judaism and Islam, by rejecting the divinity of Christ cannot, by definition, be a part of a unity that Jesus Christ Himself declared to be dependent upon His oneness with God the Father.

I cannot have fellowship with the true God and reject His divinity in Christ at the same time. This is not my teaching but the message of Jesus, the One who said in the same gospel, *"I am the way and the truth and the life; no one comes to the Father but through Me."* (John 14:6).

This is the truth we have already seen declared in Jesus' prayer: first, that the world would know that the Father sent Jesus, His followers must be united ... *"... that they may be one ..."*; and second, that it would be a unity patterned after the communion of the Trinity ... *"... just as We are one."*

So what is the pattern of unity that is revealed in the Trinity? How was it demonstrated by Jesus in practice?

We will look at the Holy Spirit shortly, but let's start with the Father and the Son. What did Jesus mean when He said, *"I and the Father are one"*? (John 10:30)

One with the Father

John's Gospel is rich in Jesus' description of His unity with His

Father. Here are some examples ...

> *"... 'Truly, truly, I say to you, the Son can do nothing of Himself, unless it is something He sees the Father doing; for whatever the Father does, these things the Son also does in like manner. For the Father loves the Son, and shows Him all things that He Himself is doing; and the Father will show Him greater works than these, so that you will marvel.'"* John 5:19-20

> *"'I do nothing on My own initiative, but I speak these things as the Father taught Me. And He who sent Me is with Me; He has not left Me alone, for I always do the things that are pleasing to Him.'"* John 8:28-29

> *"'For I did not speak on My own initiative, but the Father Himself who sent Me has given Me a commandment as to what to say and what to speak. I know that His commandment is eternal life; therefore the things I speak, I speak just as the Father has told Me.'"* John 12:49-50

> *"'... He who has seen Me has seen the Father ...'"* John 14:9

... And so on.

Jesus could not have been clearer. He never once spoke an original word or performed an independent act. The One through whom John's Gospel tells us all creation was spoken into being (John 1:3), never operated exclusively out of His own, private initiative.

Before creation began, but revealed for us during that brief pocket of time between the beginning and end of Jesus' earthly ministry, this is the same Jesus who was sent by the Father and the Spirit into His wilderness testing; who spent the night in divine consultation before selecting His twelve disciples; and who ultimately surrendered to the will of His Father in Gethsemane with the words, *"Not My will, but Yours be done."*

It was because Jesus never did anything 'off His own bat' that the rejection of Him was the same as rejecting God the Father. Jesus said this Himself, much to the chagrin of the Pharisees.

Perhaps some have a wrong mental contrast between the Father and the Son, seeing them as being in some way different from each other in nature and purpose. One faulty image people have is of God the Father as an angry judge ready to punish, while Jesus represents God's compassionate, protective side, shielding us from a remote, dispassionate judge by His sacrificial death.

Such imaginations create differences between the Father and the Son, failing to appreciate that every aspect of the Son's ministry was the Father's idea, that they have eternally lived in perfect harmony of nature and purpose. Traits such as mercy and empathy are wrongly ascribed exclusively to Jesus; conversely, wrath and justice are detached from Jesus, with the likes of Jesus' cleansing of the temple and His graphic descriptions of Hell airbrushed out of the picture!

Read again and discover afresh that all of God is fully revealed in Jesus! John's Gospel is very clear that everything Jesus did was the Father's work. Jesus' life and ministry on earth was the exact representation of His Father's heart and mind.

Luke affirms the same truth in Acts 10:38 when he writes, *"... [Jesus] went about doing good, and healing all who were oppressed by the devil;* **for God was with Him**.*"* (Emphasis mine) God the Father was the One behind everything God the Son did, the source of all Jesus' mercy and empathy. Everything Jesus gave to us, He gave to us for His Father's sake.

And what did God the Son pray? He interceded that His followers would be one, just as He and the Father are one.

This is all sound, orthodox biblical theology. Now, let's make some practical application.

The Trinity knows nothing of independence

There is a sense of dysfunction when Christians assertively describe their local church as 'independent'. I say this as someone whose earliest Christian experience was in a vibrant city church where some of us, myself included, described ourselves as 'an independent church'. (Whisper it ... separated from the errors of 'dead denominations and churches' out there - I later came to identify a denomination as simply an independent church that got big).

The same dysfunction of independence exists with whole denominations when they emphasise their exclusivity from the wider Christian church, sometimes to the point of defining themselves by what they are 'not' rather than what they 'are', spending an inordinate amount of time justifying their 'distinctives' rather than celebrating the wonderful truths foundational to the entire body of Christ. In fairness, such denominationalism was probably part of the reason my friends and I embraced 'independence', seeing it as the only alternative.

But the truth is, both industrial-scale and small-sized independence are at odds with the One who repeatedly stressed that He did 'nothing of His own initiative', who lived and served in collaboration with the Trinity.

When my so-called movement whiffs of exclusivity, the idea that we have everything to offer the wider church but nothing to learn from it, we exhibit the same dysfunction as any small-corner, independent church.

The same principle fundamentally applies, of course, to individual Christians when we think we can live healthy Christian lives outside of fellowship with a local body of believers. 'You don't need to go to church to be a Christian,' goes the far-too-unchallenged claim.

Jesus' prayer made it clear that I cannot be a healthy Christian outside of community. I cannot touch Jesus without engaging meaningfully and habitually with the community He has fully identified with and ascribed His name to, as the 'body of Christ.' Over the centuries, countless Christians have walked out of churches where Jesus Himself has continued to show up.

"May they be one," Jesus prayed, *"just as We are one."*

As Paul wrote in his analogy of the church as Christ's body in I Corinthians 12:14-27, no part of the body can say of any other part that it doesn't need it. What is this, if it is not the outworking of Jesus' prayer, that the same unity and loving inter-dependence binding Him to His Father would now be put to work among His followers. The world would now know that they were His disciples, by the love they had for one another - love that never fails (tires), even when bitterly challenged.

Jesus never once lived or acted as an independent agent. It took a Roman soldier to articulate this most clearly:

> *"But the centurion said, 'Lord, I am not worthy for You to come under my roof, but just say the word, and my servant will be healed. For I **also** am a man under authority, with soldiers under me; and I say to this one, "Go!" and he goes, and to another, "Come!" and he comes, and to my slave, "Do this!" and he does it.' Now when Jesus heard this, He marvelled and said to those who were following, 'Truly I say to you, I have not found such great faith with anyone in Israel."'* Mat-

thew 8:8-10 (Emphasis mine)

The centurion was a man of great faith. He was also a man of understanding. Note the word 'also' that says so much. The implication was that he saw a clear parallel between himself carrying the authority of Caesar, and Jesus carrying the full authority of God the Father. To resist the Centurion was to resist Caesar. When the Centurion commanded, the imperial might of Rome spoke. The centurion understood that Jesus' word was God Himself speaking; that Jesus was not operating out of His own personal source any more than he was.

In the same way as the perfect success of Jesus' earthly ministry was the outflow of His unity with the Father, so the success of the church's mission, if Jesus' prayer is to be believed, depends upon our unity with Christ, a unity that is manifested on earth by His followers' unity with one another in Him.

This unity is enabled by the Third Person of the Trinity, the Holy Spirit, who is now in and with Jesus' followers on earth. Jesus' pattern is the Spirit's pattern too.

Another Helper

Jesus said that the Holy Spirit would operate out of the same divine unity as He did. In John chapter 14, the discourse shifts from His own unity with the Father to that of the Holy Spirit, using the same terminology.

Jesus prepares His disciples for this in response to Philip's request that Jesus show them the Father ...

> *"... He who has seen Me has seen the Father; how can you say, "Show us the Father"? Do you not believe that I am in the Father, and the Father is in Me? The words that I say to you I do not speak on My own initiative,*

*but the Father abiding in Me does His works. Believe Me that I am in the Father and the Father is in Me; otherwise believe because of the works themselves. Truly, truly, I say to you, he who believes in Me, the works that I do, he will do also; and greater works than these he will do; **because I go to the Father**.'"* John 14:9-12 (Emphasis mine)

What was going to happen when Jesus went to the Father? Jesus soon explains:

*"'I will ask the Father, and He will give you **another Helper**, that He may be with you forever.'"* John 14:16 (Emphasis mine)

The original New Testament has two Greek words for 'another': *allos* and *heteros. Allos* refers to another of the same kind and *heteros* to another of a different kind. If you were sitting at a table holding a knife and asked me for another, using the word *'heteros',* I might offer you a fork or a spoon. But if you used the word *'allos',* I should give you another knife, another of the *same kind.*

When Jesus identified the Spirit as *"another Helper,"* He used the word *'allos';* in other words, Another of the same kind as Himself!

"'But when He, the Spirit of truth, comes, He will guide you into all the truth; for He will not speak on His own initiative, but whatever He hears, He will speak.'" John 16:13

The Holy Spirit was going to lead the disciples into the same union with Jesus and the Father as Jesus Himself had with the Father.

Little wonder Jesus went on to tell the disciples it was to their advantage that He go away! (John 16:7) Up until now, their personal connection to God was limited to His physical presence, and their empowerment depended upon their hearing and obeying Jesus' - and, therefore, the Father's - instructions while they were with Him.

When the Holy Spirit came, His presence would be the equivalent of Jesus simultaneously and permanently being with every one of them, wherever they went. The Holy Spirit would ever be there to answer their questions; to reveal God, His word and His ways; to give them His instructions; to show them 'how to do it' (and how not to).

This is why Jesus' ministry would explode on earth after Pentecost, after His ascension to 'mission control' at the right hand of the Father ... "... *head over all things to the church.*" (Ephesians 1:22)

The Holy Spirit, just like Jesus, would not speak independently of Jesus and the Father, but from the one essence of the Trinity, just as Jesus had.

> *"'All things that the Father has are Mine [Son]; therefore I said that He [Holy Spirit] takes of Mine and will disclose it to you.'"* John 16:15

There we see it: the Trinity in action, displaying the kind of unity that, if replicated in us, will enable the world to see God the Father in Christ in the Spirit ... in us.

In the same way as Jesus exemplified unity by His Oneness with the Father, the Holy Spirit, now dwelling in His followers, operates out of His unity with the Son and the Father.

Everyone who truly embraces the Holy Spirit is necessarily in unity not only with the Spirit but with the Trinity, but also with everyone else who embraces the same Holy Spirit, fulfilling Jesus' prayer, *"that they may be one, just as We are one."*

The unity of the Spirit

Listen to the words of Paul's benediction: *"The grace of the Lord Jesus Christ, and the love of God, and **the fellowship of the Holy Spirit**, be with you all."* (II Corinthians 13:14, emphasis mine)

That word 'fellowship' is, in its modern usage, a soft translation of the Greek, *koinonia,* which speaks of a deeply binding communion that flows out of a commonality of source. The fellowship of the Spirit demonstrated in Christ's body is exactly what Jesus prayed for, an expression of the same union that has eternally existed within the Trinity.

Understanding this is the key to understanding John's seemingly unfathomable statement in I John 4:17: *"... as He is, so also are we in this world."*

"As He is"?

But how *is* He?

This is the same chapter that twice declares, *"God is love,"* and distinguishes the true Spirit (or, the Spirit of truth) from a false spirit, by the great hallmark of love. This love, demonstrated by the unity of God's people, is what reveals those who truly belong to Christ.

Wonderfully, this passage also explains why God has to be a Trinity. If God is love, and if God is eternal, then love must have existed before creation.

And love cannot exist without an object, without another to love. Three Persons, Father, Son and Holy Spirit, have forever loved each other. As He is, so also are we in this world: a loving community. The context of I John 4:17 makes it very clear that this is what John is talking about.

We read on, in verses 16 and 17:

> "... God is love, and the one who abides in love abides in God, and God abides in him. By this, love is perfected with us, so that we may have confidence in the day of judgement; because as He is, so also are we in this."

The love of the eternal Trinity, demonstrated by our harmonious participation in Christ's body, gives us personal confidence for our eternal future.

Note also that word 'perfected' (also translated 'matured'). It is exactly the same word prayed by Jesus:

> "... That they may be one, just as We are one; I in them and You in Me, that they may be **perfected** in unity, so that the world may know that You sent Me." (Emphasis mine)

The work of perfecting, or maturing, us in unity is the ministry of the Third Person of the Trinity. Jesus may not be here physically to wash our feet and teach us how to prefer one another, but He did say the Holy Spirit would be just like Him; that He would "... bring to your remembrance all that I said to you." (John 14:26)

The Holy Spirit is the One who matures the church in the unity of God the Trinity, the One of whom Paul teaches the Ephesians:

> "... being diligent to preserve the unity of the Spirit in the bond of peace." Ephesians 4:3

Paul goes straight on to declare the work of the Spirit:

> *"There is one body and one Spirit, just as also you were called in one hope of your calling; one Lord, one faith, one baptism, one God and Father of all who is over all and through all and in all."* Ephesians 4:4-6

Just like Jesus, the Holy Spirit has perfect unity with the Father and the Son. He is able to mature us in this very unity when we receive Him. He is the One who outworks the Father's answer to Jesus' prayer for our unity, thus empowering our witness on earth:

> *"By this all men will know that you are My disciples, if you have love for one another."* John 13:35

It is because Jesus came that we are able to see, hear and know all these things. It is through Him, and Him alone, that we who believe - and all who believe through us - will begin to see The Big Picture:

> *All of Christ in All the Church to All Creation.*

PART I: ALL OF CHRIST

3. REVEALING GOD

*"For in Him all the fullness of
Deity dwells in bodily form."*

Colossians 2:9

The New Testament is very clear about who Jesus is. Beyond question, He is more than a man. Paul's letter to the Colossians presents Him as preeminent over all things, the divine Son of God in whose body dwells the fullness of Deity or, as the King James Bible puts it, the fullness of the Godhead.

A big picture of *'All of Christ'* neither excludes the other Persons of the Trinity nor elevates the Son of God above Them; on the contrary, it is in Him that all Three are most clearly seen. It is in Jesus that we know God. The Godhead have made Themselves known to mankind through the Son of God who became a man, entering the human race as the earthly representative of the Holy Trinity. To zero on Jesus is to embrace and magnify the fullness of the Trinity, not to underplay or conceal Them.

When the Word became flesh, the invisible God was made manifest so that all eyes on Earth could now see, and every human mind could know, what God is like by looking at Jesus.

As John put in his First Epistle, *"What ... we have heard, what we have seen with our eyes, what we have looked at and touched with our hands, concerning the Word of Life ... What we have seen and heard we proclaim to you ..."* (I John 1:1, 3)

We could never personally know God had the Son not become a man. Before Christ, God was untouchable by humanity. *"No man shall see Me, and live,"* God had told Moses (Exodus 33:20). And thus it was, until the Second Person of the Trinity took on an 'earth suit' and lit up human history: *"And the Word became flesh, and dwelt among us, and we saw His glory, glory as of the only begotten from the Father, full of grace and truth."* (John 1:14)

As Paul again puts it, *"It was the Father's good pleasure for all the fulness to dwell in Him."* (Colossians 1:19)

There is nothing of the essence and nature of God the Father that is not embodied and appreciable in the God the Son, Jesus Christ. Co-equal with the Father and the Holy Spirit, Christ the Son, in His essence, is eternal and infinite, uncaused and unchanging, Creator and Sustainer of all things. In His nature, He is perfect in holiness and justice, love and goodness, faithfulness and truth. All the attributes and virtues of God are fully His.

The writer to the Hebrews describes Him as *"the radiance of His glory and the exact representation of His glory."* (Hebrews 1:3) Little wonder this same writer later speaks of *"fixing our eyes upon Jesus."* (Hebrews 12:2). Anything we could wish to know about God is to be discovered by looking on Him. The true Light having come into the world, we are no longer in the dark as to what God is like. Every time we ask the question, *'What would Jesus do?'* we affirm the phenomenal revelatory truth that the will of God is now within human reach through Jesus.

In His humanity, Jesus did serve the role of an earthly prophet, to be sure, but to see only the holy man and not the divine Son is to filter out what He said about Himself and to be a stranger to the essence of who Jesus really is. Yes, He is the Friend of sinners, but He is also both the Creator of the universe, and the One for Whom the universe was created. He does not come in two packages, one human and the other divine, a kind of hybrid half-God-half-human; He is fully human and fully divine, and we cannot truly have one without the other.

As C. S. Lewis famously put it in his 1940s BBC radio broadcasts, *"Let us not come with any patronising nonsense about his being a great human teacher."* A man, Lewis continued, who said the sort of things Jesus said about Himself either was who He said He was - the eternal Son of God - or he was a liar, a madman or something worse. We must choose between these options as they are the only ones available.

The Epistle to the Hebrews, just like the Gospel of John and the Epistle to the Colossians, puts Jesus on another level than the prophets, even the venerated Moses: *"For [Jesus] has been counted worthy of more glory than Moses, by just so much as the builder of the house has more honour than the house."* (Hebrews 3:3)

Moses, we read in Exodus, was sent to Pharaoh *by* the I AM; Jesus, on the other hand, claimed to *be* the I AM, greater than the most eminent of prophets such as Moses and Abraham. The Jews of Jesus' day resisted this violently, seeking to stone Him for blasphemy when He claimed, *"Before Abraham was, I AM!"* (John 8:58)

According to Jesus, there had never been a greater human being than his physically older cousin, John the Baptist (Matthew 11:11). And yet John considered himself unworthy even of tying the thong of Jesus' sandals, saying, *"This is He on behalf of whom I said, 'After me comes a Man who has a higher rank than I, for He existed before me.'"* (John 1:30)

Greater than prophets, teachers and evangelists who could never be anything more than useful prototypes of The One to come: *"... Something greater than Jonah is here,"* (Matthew 12:41) Jesus told the Jews.

Greater than the wisest of the wise: *"... Behold, something greater than Solomon is here."* (Matthew 12:42)

Holier than the holiest things on earth: *"Something greater than the temple is here."* (Matthew 12:6)

Higher than angelic beings: *"... To which of the angels has He ever said, 'Sit at My right hand, until I make Your enemies a footstool for Your feet'?"* (Hebrews 1:13)

Outstanding in its revelation of the divinity of Jesus Christ is the Gospel of John, the Book of the Seven I AMs and of the Seven Signs, each miracle selected as a spotlight upon the divine attributes of Jesus.

Merrill C. Tenney, in *John: The Gospel of Belief*, writes that when Jesus turns water into wine, He is the Master of Quality; when He heals the nobleman's son by a word from afar, He is the Master of Distance; when He heals a paralytic of 38 years, He is the Master of Time; when He feeds the 5,000, He is the Master of Quantity; when He walks on the water, He is the Master of Natural Law; when He heals a man ill-fated to be born blind, He is the Master of Misfortune; and when He conquers the ultimate foe by raising Lazarus from the tomb, He is the Master of Death.

These signs, for believer and unbeliever alike, are the embodiment of the I AM who is Jesus Christ, Son of God, Second Person of the Trinity. Jesus Himself said, *"I told you, and you do not believe; the works that I do in My Father's name, these testify of Me."* (John 10:25) Anyone deaf to the words of Jesus would need to be blind not to see His works, the visible demonstrations of the divinity He claimed.

The One who said, *"I am the true vine"* (15:1) is He who turned water into wine. The One who said *"I am the bread of life"* (6:48) is He who fed 5,000 with five loaves. The One who said, *"I am the Light of the World"* (8:12) is He who opened the eyes of the man born blind. The One who said *"I am the Resurrection and the Life"* (11:25) is He who raised Lazarus from the tomb.

He didn't just *say*, *"I am the Door of the Sheep,"* (10:7) *"I am the Good Shepherd,"* (10:11) and *"I am the Way, and the Truth, and the Life;"* (14:6) He actually *became* all of these things to all who would simply receive Him by believing.

The sixty-six books of the Bible amount to the narration of God's redemption plan for a fallen world, and in that great story the Person of Jesus Christ is the central and uniting theme. God Himself enters human history in the body of the man, Jesus Christ, the prophesied one, to reconcile the children of Adam to the God for Whom they were created.

John introduces the Son as *"the true Light which, coming into the world, enlightens every man. He was in the world, and the world was made through Him, and the world did not know Him. He came to His own, and those who were His own did not receive Him. But as many as received Him, to them He gave the right to become children of God, even to those who believe in His name, who were born, not of blood nor of the will of the flesh nor of the will of man, but of God."* (John 1:9-13)

What a story! God became a man to bring mankind into the family of God, into the household of the One in whose image they alone were created. The Son of God became the Son of Man so that sons of men might become sons of God.

Everything in the Old Testament was types and shadows, silhouettes and paintings, maps and directions. But in Jesus Christ, God Himself arrives personally and takes centre stage. Those who receive Jesus Christ as the Son of God, as one with the Father and the Holy Spirit, no longer simply know *of* God, they now **know** Him ... *"No one has seen God at any time; the only begotten God who is in the bosom of the Father, He has explained Him."* (John 1:18)

The divine Son of God dazzles us in a series of personal encounters on the pages of John's Gospel. The Eternal One discloses

Himself to a frowned-upon Samaritan woman, to whom Jesus declares (original Greek), *"Ego eimi ho lalon soi"* - literally, *"I AM the speaking one to you!"* (4:26)

Or to detested Roman soldiers, demonstrating that He was even in charge of His own arrest, trial and crucifixion. When He introduced Himself again as *"Ego eimi"* (I AM), *"… they drew back and fell to the ground."* (18:6)

It is beyond our mental capacity to understand *how* God, the Creator of all things, could possibly become an object of His own creation; *how* the Eternal One could be contained in a human body within which *"all the fullness of the Godhead dwelt."* (Colossians 2:9)

Not even the most developed human intelligences can begin to grasp the infinite. I recently heard cosmologist Katie Mack confess, *"I have never been able to get my head round how some infinities can be bigger than others."* Listening to her speak, my smaller mind sympathised. How can one thing possibly be bigger than another thing that is already infinitely big? And yet, as Mack admitted, theoretical physicists, in good faith, continue to calculate on the assumption that infinities do come in an infinite number of different sizes!

When even the great start to contemplate the infinite, their brains become smaller than the tiniest of microscopic molecules, and any true scientist will be the first to admit this (- militant atheists ought to consider the correlation between humility and true learning!).

For the infinite, read Divine. No theologian can begin to explain the *how* of one of the most basic of Christian doctrines: the incarnation – the Eternal One fully embodied in a human frame. No Bible scholar can explain *how* God could become a man, but the New Testament is very clear, not just *that* He did but *why* He did.

He came to reveal God to His creation; to make the Father knowable to us by looking upon, and listening to, the Son.

So, what will *you* do with Jesus?

Imagine even asking you such a question! How can it be that the divine Son of God should give *you* the power to decide what to do with *Him?!*

Yet He does.

The world He speaks into being. The waves He stops. Blinds eyes He opens. The dead He raises. It seems that the human will is the only thing on earth to which He grants the power to say *'No!'* to Him, and it is a power that, ever since Adam and Eve, we have made much use of. But for us to have been created in God's own image meant for us to have genuinely free will.

In John chapter 6, the storm-tossed disciples had been rowing for up to four miles when suddenly the Master of the Elements appeared walking on the water. Moments later, having introduced Himself as *"I AM"*, He stands on board and, from the wording of the text, appears to teleport the boat instantly to the side of the lake!

But read what the Omnipotent One subjects Himself to in the middle of the story: "... *So* **they were willing** *to receive Him into the boat ...*" (6:21, emphasis mine) *They* were willing! Yes, the Sovereign of all things and Master of the elements gives those He created the power to receive or reject Him, and condescends to await their invitation before stepping onto the humble craft produced from the very elements He Himself had formed in the beginning.

What was resistible to their wills was irresistible to their hearts, and they chose wisely.

So, what will *you* do with Jesus?

Will you welcome Him into your 'boat', not just into the generality of life, but into the anxieties of the storms, to your emotional struggles and the turmoil of relational conflict.

The One who walks on water and supersedes the natural world awaits the invitation to board your vessel. But know this: He doesn't come to 'help out'; He comes to captain the craft.

What will *you* do with such an awesome Person?

4. REDEEMING MANKIND

"The next day [John the Baptist] saw Jesus coming and said, 'Behold, the Lamb of God who takes away the sin of the world.'"

John 1:29

How amazing that God should unveil Himself to us in human flesh! But Jesus came to do more than reveal God: He came to redeem mankind.

The revelation of God and the redemption of man are embodied in one person, Jesus Christ, and are frequently celebrated in the same breath of Scripture:

> *"He had equal status with God but didn't think so much of himself that he had to cling to the advantages of that status no matter what. Not at all. When the time came, he set aside the privileges of deity and took on the status of a slave, became human! Having become human, he stayed human. It was an incredibly humbling process. He didn't claim special privileges. Instead, he lived a selfless, obedient life and then died a selfless, obedient death – and the worst kind of death at that – a crucifixion."* Philippians 2:5-8 (The

Message)

Bible scholars are rightly swift to point out that this Jesus is no half-God-half-man hybrid. No, He is fully God *and* fully man! Eternal Sovereign and earthly sacrifice in one run of the Bible-writer's pen.

In John's Gospel, John the Baptist identifies Jesus as the Pre-existent One immediately after introducing Him as the sacrificial Lamb whose death would pay for the sins of humanity. (John 1:29-30)

In Hebrews, Jesus is the radiance and representation of the Divine who *"upholds all things by the word of His power."* ... And then, in the same verse: *"... He made purification of sins."* (1:3)

In Colossians, Paul begins, *"... It was the Father's good pleasure for all the fullness to dwell in Him ..."* before continuing, *"... and through Him to reconcile all things to Himself, having made peace through the blood of the cross ..."* (1: 19-20)

In the same breath: Son of God *and* Son of Man.

The Bible is God's plan of redemption for a world corrupted by the sin of Adam, needing to be reconciled to God and restored to its creation purpose. Human redemption required a substitute who was fully man. Yet it had to be a perfect, unblemished 'lamb', one who would not only take man's sin but, in exchange, provide God's righteousness.

Only a human being uncontaminated by the sin of Adam could pay the price. And so came Jesus, born of a woman, yet conceived not of Joseph, but of the Holy Spirit, and fully divine, the perfect embodiment of God. One mediator who would forever remain God and man.

Jesus was the One prophesied by Isaiah, with *"no stately form or majesty"* (Isaiah 53:2), *"tempted in all things as we are, yet without sin,"* (Hebrews 4:15), who would take upon His body the sin, guilt and judgement of a fallen race.

To think that the following Gospel message was preached some seven centuries before Jesus' arrival! ...

> *"He was pierced through for our transgressions, He was crushed for our iniquities; the chastening for our well-being fell upon Him, and by His scourging we are healed. All of us like sheep have gone astray, each of us has turned to his own way; but the Lord has caused the iniquity of us all to fall on Him. He was oppressed and He was afflicted, yet He did not open His mouth; like a lamb that is led to slaughter, and like a sheep that is silent before its shearers, so He did not open His mouth ... Cut off out of the land of the living for the transgression of my people, to whom the stroke was due ..."* Isaiah 53:5-8

Roll forward the centuries to the other side of the centre of history, to the other side of the cross, and listen to the apostle Paul:

> *"In Him we have redemption through His blood, the forgiveness of our trespasses, according to the riches of His grace which He lavished on us."* Ephesians 1:7-8

In Him we have redemption! But what *is* redemption?

Redemption is the reconciliation of everything corrupted by sin back to God, the rescue of the original divine purpose. The reversal of the Fall and the restoration of the Fallen, purchased by the blood of the Lamb, Jesus Christ.

The awesome truth of redemption is that, not only did Christ's blood pay for sin, it also dealt with the consequences. The scope of Christ's redeeming work is cosmic, extending to anything that has, in any way, directly or indirectly, been affected by

Adam's sin.

In a day yet to come, the purchase of Christ's once-for-all sacrifice will finally be consummated in the delivery from above of a New Heaven and a New Earth (Revelation 21-22). As Howard Snyder wrote (2004, *The Community of the King*), fallen man may be the centre of redemption, but the circumference extends to every created thing, spiritual and physical, in the heavens and on earth.

In Part 3 of *The Big Picture*, we will consider the cosmic scope of God's plan of redemption and, therefore, Christ's and the Church's sphere of influence. But for now, let Paul's message to the Colossians begin to percolate on the 'back burner' of our minds:

> "*... It was the Father's good pleasure for all the fulness to dwell in Him, and through Him to reconcile **all things** to Himself, having made peace through the blood of His cross; through Him, I say, **whether things on earth or things in heaven**.*" Colossians 1:19-20 (Emphasis mine)

But let's start at the centre. Redemption begins where sin entered and the Fall took place: in the hearts, minds and wills of Eve and of Adam, those created in the image of God, to whom God had entrusted stewardship of His creation.

Man's relationship with God was breached by sin. The fabric of fellowship with God was torn. As Isaiah explained to the people of his day, "*... Your iniquities have made a separation between you and your God, and your sins have hidden His face from you so that He does not hear.*" (59:2)

It was this chasm that only the blood of God's unblemished Lamb could repair. And repair it He did! It is a revolutionary truth that when Jesus died on the cross, He not only bore our sinful nature but imputed to our account His own righteousness, or right-standing with God. What an exchange!

In His body, Jesus reconciled the balance sheet by accounting for our sin, and thus ended our separation from God. By faith, those who receive Jesus Christ as God's sacrificial Lamb are justified, or - if I may vandalise the English language - righteous-ified.

... Declared righteous!

If there seems to be any unfairness in all humanity being condemned by the sin of Adam, in whose seed was all humanity, then how unfair is it that the believer should be declared clean on merit of Jesus' righteousness!

This is the good news of redemption in Jesus Christ: all who receive Christ the Lamb by faith are now declared righteous, by His blood not their effort:

> *"For if by the transgression of the one, death reigned through the one, much more those who receive the abundance of grace and of the **gift of righteousness** will reign in life through the One, Jesus Christ. So then as through one transgression there resulted condemnation to all men, even so **through one act of righteousness there resulted justification of life to all men.**"* Romans 5:17-18 (Emphases mine)

There we have it: the *gift* of righteousness!

Because of the sacrifice of the Lamb of God, the sinner is by faith made righteous, freely pardoned and exonerated as an unearned gift! What an affront to our best religious efforts! Where is the room for pride and self-righteousness in that?

A free gift, yet provided at the greatest cost imaginable: the substitutionary death of the Son of God, Jesus Christ.

What an astounding revelation: *"[God] made Him who knew no sin to be sin on our behalf, so that we might become the righteousness of God in Him."* (II Corinthians 5:21)

What a Gospel!

As a young child, I was catechised by the Westminster Confession of Faith. Question 18 required of me no small feat, to memorise the answer to the following question: *"Wherein consisteth the sinfulness of that estate whereinto man fell?"*

My exhausting answer, nearly 50 years later, is by memory: *"The sinfulness of that estate whereinto man fell consists in the guilt of Adam's first sin, the want of original righteousness and the corruption of his whole nature, which is commonly called original sin, together with all actual transgressions which proceed from it."*

Well!

Original sin is a fact. And, I hasten to add, it's an indispensable foundational fact of the Christian creed. But it's only half the truth.

My difficulty with the Catechism is not what's in it, but what's left out!

Having dealt in such detail with sin, why did the authors not follow Paul's example in Romans chapter 5, and flow seamlessly onto the good news about righteousness? While I don't suggest they should have dropped the doctrine of sin, is righteousness not something better to be writing about?

Why not a Question 18b, something along the lines of: *Wherein consisteth the **righteousness** of that estate whereinto the **believer** was **raised**?*

Here might be Paul's answer: *The righteousness of that estate wherinto the believer was raised consists in the merit of Christ's obedient act, His substitutionary death for sin and His gift of right-standing with God, which is commonly called justification by faith, together with all good works which proceed from it.*

What a Gospel! Jesus Christ came to declare sinners righteous. And so much more follows on from that.

The wonder of the redemption story is that Jesus Christ's sacrificial death not only justifies those who believe in Him, it also brings those who receive Him into a status of adoption as children of God.

> *"... As many as received Him, to them He gave the right to become children of God, even to those who believe in His name."* John 1:12

... Children of God!

Not servants of the law or slaves to performance as a means of status before God, but children and heirs by adoption. Since believers' sins have been legally paid for, there is no longer any impediment to their entry to the family of God.

> *"... Having forgiven us all our transgressions, having cancelled out the certificate of debt consisting of decrees against us, which was hostile to us; ... He has taken it out of the way, having nailed it to the cross."* Colossians 2:13-14

Having dealt with sin, adoption into God's holy family is now possible. Paul taught that it had all been planned in advance:

> *"[God] predestined us to adoption as sons through Jesus Christ to Himself, according to the kind intention of His will."* Ephesians 1:5

Paul's illustration of adoption is a powerful picture of the relationship between God and the Christian. In Roman Law at the time Paul wrote, it was a commonly understood legal fact that an adopted child held the same rights of status and inheritance as a biological child.

Again, Paul writes to the Galatians:

> *"For you are all sons of God through faith in Christ Jesus."* (3:26)

And to the Romans:

> *"... You have received a spirit of adoption as sons by which we cry out, 'Abba! Father!'"* (8:15)

Adopted. But there's more, so much more!

Jesus' blood paid for even more than our righteousness and our adoption: it actually prepared the way for God's indwelling presence within the believer. The believer's son-ship is more than one of legal right: it is one of spiritual substance.

God's redeemed people, the church, each believer individually and the entire community collectively, have become the dwelling place of the Holy Spirit. Jesus' blood provided for the Christian's regeneration, or new birth, by the Spirit of God living within.

We are reborn, or 'born from above', by the Holy Spirit Himself. The *"imperishable seed"* (I Peter 1:23) of God's word having been conceived in the believing heart, a new creature is birthed, described by Paul as *"... the new man, which in the likeness of God has been created in righteousness and holiness of the truth."* (Ephesians 4:24)

The born again believer is not just a legal child of God, but the **actual** spiritual offspring of God, with God's spiritual DNA now dwelling within!

This is what it means to become a Christian: not an improved or recycled version of the old, but a brand new person by spiritual birth, a child of Heaven.

> *"Therefore if anyone is in Christ, he is a new creature; the old things passed away; behold, new things have come."* II Corinthians 5:17

Every aspect of redemption - whether justification, adoption or regeneration - is entirely the work of Jesus Christ and all the glory goes to Him, leaving no room for pride or human boasting ...

> *"... **By His doing** you are in Christ Jesus, who became to us wisdom from God, and righteousness and sanctification, and redemption, so that, just as it is written, 'Let him who boasts, boast in the Lord.'"* I Corinthians 1:30-31 (Emphasis mine)

Note yet another treasure of redemption: sanctification!

Some Christians have been sold the idea that sanctification is **our** work, a religious climb to an eventual state of sinless perfection on the journey of life, a pilgrimage to be trudged through, with a sense of shame and inadequacy, by all but perhaps a godly few. Those who seem to make less of a hash of it than others are sometimes referred to as 'saints' ('sanctified ones' in short).

Nothing could be further from the truth: sanctification, just like every other wonder of redemption, is Jesus Christ's work entirely! He is the Sanctifier; the believer is the sanctified.

Yes, sanctification demands the believer's response. Absolutely! But it is only because the believer has been justified by faith and regenerated by the Spirit that he or she gets to participate in the outworking. Sanctification literally means 'set apart unto' and it is a starting point rather than a finishing point.

Having been set apart, as justified believers, as adopted children of God indwelt by the Holy Spirit, Christians are empowered to participate in outworking the salvation to which they have been separated. Paul urged the Philippians to *"work out your salvation with fear and trembling,"* (2:12) but there is an eternity of a difference between working ***out*** your salvation and working ***for*** your salvation - Paul's sentence continues: *"... for it is God who is at work in you, both to will and to work for His good pleasure."* (v. 13)

As with justification, sanctification (true sainthood) is earned and provided only by Jesus' completed work on the cross, as the writer to the Hebrews points out:

> *"... It was fitting for Him, for whom are all things, and through whom are all things, in bringing many sons to glory, to perfect the author of their salvation through sufferings. For both He who sanctifies and those who are sanctified are all from one Father ..."* Hebrews 2:10-11

"... He who sanctifies and those who are sanctified ..." It is very clear who is the one doing the sanctifying.

Notice how Paul's letters address the Christians in Rome, Ephesus, Philippi and Colossae. He identifies them as *"saints,"* not *"sinners"* - the believer's spiritual position is accomplished by the work of Christ, never the best or worst of his own efforts. Even the Corinthians, infamous for their spiritual immaturity, are identified *"saints."* (Interestingly, Paul does not use the term *"saints"* with the Galatians, who appear to have been bewitched into "another gospel" of salvation by the self-effort of religious works, rather than justification by faith in the completed work of Jesus Christ.)

Sanctification is *the work of God in setting the believer apart for a holy purpose.*

It is not a process of self-improvement that a special class of 'holy people' do well; rather, it is a work of God, with the believer the object that has been sanctified, or set apart for God's redemptive purpose.

In the Old Testament, sanctification was applied to inanimate objects such as furnishings in the temple or geographical places reserved for a holy purpose. These objects obviously have no moral value in themselves; it is the One who sets up in residence that infuses them with His perfect purity and goodness.

In the New Testament, we read, for example, that a believing spouse *"sanctifies"* their unbelieving partner (I Corinthians 7:14). This implies no spiritual or moral merit on the part of the one being sanctified - it merely indicates that the presence of a Spirit-indwelt believer sets the whole family apart for favour and blessing that the family would not otherwise know. This again illustrates that it is the One who sanctifies rather than the one being sanctified that bears merit.

The wonderful truth of redemption is that, once the believer is sanctified, he or she becomes indwelt by the Sanctifier. This is what saints are: holy instruments of sanctification wherever they go.

In the Old Testament, the tabernacle (and later the temple) was sanctified as the place of God's holy dwelling; but in the New, God's people are the temple! We are the holy (sanctified) place, set apart for the purposes of God by the redeeming work of Jesus' cross.

So Jesus came not only to reveal God, but also to redeem mankind back to God's creation intent, as His people through whom His glory would fill all creation.

So, what is the believer's response to the Redeemer who has done it all?

There is no other response than simply to say, *'Thank You!'*; to express uncontainable gratitude from the depths of our hearts. If I were to live a sinlessly perfect life for the remainder of my journey on earth, I should still be a net beneficiary of the cross of Jesus Christ, a child of grace whose only response to the clearance of my unpayable debt is to live a life of gratitude to God, and to become a channel of that same grace to a world that has no more earned it than I.

Such a response to the Redeemer is so much easier when I truly realise what Jesus Christ has done, and this is why I cannot begin to see The Big Picture until I realise who Jesus Christ is, and what He has done.

Believers who have truly seen who Jesus is and what He has done, and who have received the gift of redemption by God's grace, are the ones equipped to present their lives as such an offering. This is why Paul begins his epistles by declaring what Jesus has done, before directing the believer how to respond.

Saying *'Thank You!'*, of course, is just the beginning. The prayer might continue: *'All that You have done for me and given to me, I gladly put to work for Your glory. I don't do this to pay for my salvation - I never could - but to express my gratitude for Your unearned grace and the priceless sacrifice of Christ's blood.'*

All my good thoughts, attitudes and deeds are not me saying

'Please!' to God - they are me saying *'Thank You!'* for an immeasurable, priceless gift.

Perhaps there is no better way to worship God, to express praise and thanksgiving to Him, than to rise to Paul's challenge to the redeemed:

> *"... Lay aside the old man, which is being corrupted in accordance with the lusts of deceit, and ... be renewed in the spirit of your mind, and put on the new self, which in the likeness of God has been created in righteousness and holiness of the truth."* Ephesians 4:23-24

This we are able to do, not by our own power but by the power of the Holy Spirit.

Thank God Jesus came, bearing the revelation of God and bringing the redemption of mankind.

Can there possibly be more?

Yes - Jesus also came to raise up a people.

We cannot appreciate *'all of Christ'* without understanding His plan for us.

5. RAISING DISCIPLES

"... And He appointed twelve, so that they would be with Him and that He could send them out to preach ..."

Mark 3:14

I f Jesus came only to pay the price for sin, the mission could have been accomplished in three days. But then, who would pass on His revelation of God and the good news of His redemption to mankind after He left?

Jesus came not only as our substitute, but also as our example. And to be both substitute and example, He had to come as a man. In His humanity, Jesus both modelled and taught how his people on earth can and should be expected to live and serve Him.

It was as a man filled with the Holy Spirit that picked up the scroll in Nazareth at the outset of His ministry and announced:

> *"The Spirit of the Lord is upon Me, because He anointed Me to preach the gospel to the poor. He has sent Me to proclaim release to the captives, and recovery of sight to the blind, to set free those who are oppressed, to proclaim the favourable year of the Lord."*
> Luke 4:18-19

Earlier in the same chapter, Luke portrayed Jesus as a man

empowered by God. *"Full of the Holy Spirit,"* (verse 1) Jesus was led into the wilderness, to be tested - and to overcome - in the same areas Adam had previously failed. Then, Jesus returned to Galilee *"in the power of the Spirit,"* (verse 14) where He quoted the above words of Isaiah.

It makes perfect sense that Jesus, even though fully God, should carry out His ministry as a man filled with the Holy Spirit. How else could His followers - ordinary people - be expected to continue the same mission after His ascension to heaven?

In and of ourselves, humans cannot do what only God can do; but when the Holy Spirit comes upon us, as He came upon the man Jesus, we can do the works of God in Jesus' name.

Luke's Gospel is the account of what happened when the Holy Spirit came upon the Son of Man, Jesus Christ; Luke 'Volume 2', the Book of Acts, picks up where the Gospel leaves off, describing what happened when the Holy Spirit came upon the church just as He came upon Jesus.

Jesus' ministry of raising disciples was one of demonstration, mission assignments and teaching, and it required more than a week-end!

He spent three years equipping a team who were embryonic of what would become known as His body, the church; a community who would, in His physical absence but by the presence of the Spirit, not just deliver the words and works of God, but equip those who followed to do the same, in Jesus' name.

This was the baton Jesus passed on with the words: *"... As the Father has sent Me, I also send you."* (John 20:21)

So how had He prepared the disciples for His departure? There are three areas of discipleship that Jesus modelled for every follower: sonship, servanthood and Spirit-filled ministry.

Sonship

What is unmistakable from the Gospels is that Jesus' whole ministry flowed out of His communion with the Father. *"My food is to do the will of Him who sent Me,"* (John 4:34) He told the disciples.

Notice how He retreats to pray, often after dark or before dawn, sometimes climbing a mountain or crossing a lake to get alone with Him of Whom He said, *"I and the Father are one."* (John 10:30)

He repeatedly said that He did nothing from His own initiative; that He only spoke and did the things He heard His Father speak and saw His Father do. He lived out of total dependency upon God the Father from beginning to end, where He finally prayed, *"... Not My will, but Yours be done."* (Luke 22:42)

At the very outset, His baptism was a statement of intent to go all the way to the cross; a symbolic enactment of His death, burial and resurrection for which His course was set. Was it this agreement that moved the Father to speak from heaven, *"You are My beloved Son, in You I am well pleased."* (Luke 3:22)?

Sonship is about relationship. The Pharisees' problem was not just Jesus' claims to divinity, but His assertion of sonship; that He had a personal relationship with God which they did not have. They had religion beyond measure, but no relationship with God.

And so Jesus began His ministry by calling His disciples into relationship. *"... He appointed twelve, so that they would be with Him and that He could send them out to preach."* (Mark 3:14)

The starting point of discipleship is relationship. Jesus' order was relationship-based ministry, not ministry-based relationship.

And later, after the disciples returned from a ministry assignment, He says, *"Come away by yourselves to a secluded place and rest a while,"* and *"they went away in the boat to a secluded place by themselves."* (Mark 6:31-32)

It was by bringing the disciples into relationship with Himself that He would bring them into His relationship with the Father, and in these three years they began to experience the overflow of that relationship.

On one occasion they observed Jesus in prayer, and were so drawn by what they saw that they asked Him to teach them too ...

> *"It happened that while Jesus was praying in a certain place, after He had finished, one of His disciples said to Him, 'Lord, teach us to pray ...'"* Luke 11:1

And so, The Lord's Prayer came to us as an overspill of Jesus' relationship with the Father, firstly to the disciples and then, through them, to us.

Everything Jesus modelled and taught was an outflow of His relationship with the Father, and only out of that relationship could His work of raising disciples begin.

The relationship that Jesus had with the Father would one day be inherited by His disciples, through the Spirit who was already with them but would one day be in them; the same Spirit of sonship who now dwells in all His disciples - *"... He abides with you and will be in you,"* (John 14:17) Jesus told His disciples.

By the Holy Spirit, as Jesus Himself modelled and taught, every believer is empowered to develop a personal relationship with God, out of which to grow as disciples.

When Jesus spoke to His Father of *"I in them, and You in Me,"* (John 17:23) He was alluding to His passion to bring His disciples into the relationship with God out of which everything else flows.

When He used the parable of The Vine to illustrate the principle that apart from Him we can do nothing (John 15:5), He was simply extending to us the same principle of relational dependency upon the Vinedresser, which He Himself modelled.

When we live out of an abiding relationship with God in Christ, we bear His fruit, just as He bore His Father's fruit. This, Jesus said, is how we prove to be His disciples. (John 15:7-8)

It was out of Jesus' sonship, His relationship with the Father, that His servanthood flowed. *Relationship* is still where it all has to start. Servanthood is the next key aspect of discipleship, but sons make better servants than servants do!

And nobody better exemplified and explained what a servant is than Jesus.

Servanthood

"I am among you as the one who serves," (Luke 22:32) Jesus told His disciples.

When He washed His disciples' feet, He wasn't just serving them; He was showing them how to be servants:

> *"... If I then, the Lord and the Teacher, washed your feet, you also ought to wash one another's feet. For I gave you an example that you also should do as I did to you."* John 13:14-15

When He died on the cross, He wasn't only dying for the sins of the world; He was showing His disciples how to die. He was preparing some of them for the day their deaths would reveal His.

When the first martyr, Stephen, followed Jesus' example with the words, *"Lord, do not hold this sin against them,"* (Acts 7:60) was he not opening a window for Saul of Tarsus to see Jesus on the cross, preparing him for the heart-piercing challenge on the road to Damascus: *"Saul, Saul, why are you persecuting Me?"*? (Acts 9:4, emphasis mine)

Jesus never expressed *to* His disciples what He didn't intend to demonstrate *through* them. His works were more than an expression of His nature; they were an example for their future. His cross marked not just the end of their sins, but the start of their journey.

Jesus revealed to His disciples the character of a servant.

> *"... Whoever wishes to become great among you shall be your servant, and whoever wishes to be first among you shall be your slave; just as **the Son of Man did not come to be served, but to serve**, and to give His life a ransom for many."* Matthew 20:26-28 (Emphasis mine)

So many of Jesus's parables and teachings were about servant-hood and stewardship of the Master's resources. The great trait of the servant is faithfulness.

"Well done, good and faithful servant!" (Matthew 25:23), the good steward hears on his master's return. The faithful servant puts all he has to the best possible use, to please his master.

Jesus spelled out for His disciples what faithfulness looks like ...

> *"He who is faithful in a very little thing is faithful also in much; and he who is unrighteous in a very little thing is unrighteous also in much. Therefore if you have not been faithful in the use of unrighteous wealth, who will entrust the true riches to you? And if you have not been faithful in the use of that which is another's, who will give you that which is your own?"* Luke 16:10-12

Faithfulness with the little things, with material things, with the belongings of another ... these are the character traits of servanthood, and the marks of a disciple.

These are the very traits that Jesus exemplified Himself, only as a Son rather than a slave. His service was out of relationship: *"Moses was faithful in all his house as a servant,"* the Scriptures say, *"but Christ was faithful as a Son ..."* (Hebrews 3:5-6)

Jesus told a parable of a vineyard owner (Matthew 21:33-41) who sent two despatches of servants to collect his produce, and they were all beaten or killed. Eventually, he sent his own son - surely they would respect him? But no, they took him out and killed him, thinking they would now be able to take over the vineyard.

Jesus was clearly speaking about Himself. He is more than Moses or any of the other servants. He is the Son. He does the work of a servant and suffers as much or more than any servant, but He does so as a son.

Jesus came to raise disciples who, out of relationship with Him and with the Father, inspired by His example and His teaching, will demonstrate a servanthood that goes all the way, embraces the Father's will as its own, and is prepared to pay the ultimate price.

"It is required of stewards," Paul would later write to the Corinthians, *"that one be found faithful."* (I Corinthians 4:2)

Faithfulness is the servant-trait Paul believed qualified himself for ministry when he wrote to his disciple Timothy, *"I thank Christ Jesus our Lord, who has strengthened me, because He considered me faithful, putting me into service."* (I Timothy 1:12)

And faithfulness, not charisma, eloquence or glamour, are what Paul told Timothy to look out for in anyone else who would be entrusted the honour of serving, when he wrote,

> *"The things which you have heard from me in the presence of many witnesses, entrust these to **faithful** men who will be able to teach others also."* II Timothy

2:2 (Emphasis mine)

Little wonder, then, that when it comes time to sum up redemption history, the great conqueror riding the white horse is given the name *"Faithful and True."* (Revelation 19:11)

This is the One who came to earth on His Father's mission and stayed faithful to the end. Even when it may have seemed that all was lost, He prayed,

> *"While I was with them, I was keeping them in Your*
> *name which You have given Me; and I guarded them*
> *and not one of them perished but the son of perdition,*
> *so that the Scripture would be fulfilled."* (John 17:12)

All these uncelebrated character traits are what Jesus came to model, and to instil in the disciples He came to raise: loving sacrifice, humble stewardship, faithful endurance, and so much more.

It is so important that these two areas of discipleship - sonship (relationship) and servanthood (character) are emphasised as we consider the third area of discipleship that Jesus came to model and teach: Spirit-filled ministry.

Did Jesus not say, *"Do not rejoice in this, that the spirits are subject to you, but rejoice that your names are recorded in heaven."* (Luke 10:20)?

And didn't He warn of those who would appear before Him on Judgement Day (Matthew 7:21-23), boasting of prophesying, casting out demons and performing miracles, only to be sent away on account of their lack of both relationship (*"I never knew you"*) and character (*"You who practise lawlessness"*)?

Not all that glitters is gold.

But gold does glitter.

Once the foundations of son-ship and servanthood are in place, the raising up of disciples equipped to prophesy, cast out demons and perform miracles was very much in the package Jesus came to deliver.

Spirit-filled Ministry

Jesus made it very clear that the spiritual power demonstrated in His ministry was to accompany His followers also.

His disciples should display not only son-ship and servanthood, but the anointing of the Holy Spirit upon their words and works. The Gospel message was to be spoken in boldness and confirmed by signs following, just as it was with Him.

These phenomena were not an optional extra for Jesus' disciples, any more than they were for Him - He spoke and acted as He did because of what He saw the Father saying and doing.

> *"You know of Jesus of Nazareth, how God anointed Him with the Holy Spirit and with power, and how He went about doing good and healing all who were oppressed by the devil, **for God was with Him**."* Acts 10:38 (Emphasis mine)

Jesus did what He did because *"God was with Him."* His words and His works, as we have seen from John's Gospel, were the Father's idea, expressions of the will of God and an outflow of the relationship between Father, and Son.

The Father's heart has not changed. Jesus has not changed, and neither has the Spirit, the Other-of-the same as Jesus and the Father, the One Who is upon Jesus' disciples as He was upon Jesus.

As well as honing godly character in His disciples, Jesus was also training them to do His works. He never hid His intention ...

> *"... He who believes in Me, the works that I do, he will*

do also; and greater works than these he will do; because I go to the Father." John 14:12

There would come a day when the ascended Jesus would baptise His disciples with the Holy Spirit and, through them, the world would receive 'more of the same.' With that day in mind, Jesus' ministry was a season of preparation for when they would take up the mantle.

Jesus began with twelve ...

> *"And He called the twelve together, and gave them power and authority over all the demons and to heal diseases. And He sent them out to proclaim the kingdom of God and to perform healing ... Departing, they began going throughout the villages, preaching the gospel and healing everywhere.'" Luke 9:1-2, 6*

He then shifted gear to seventy ...

> *"Now after this the Lord appointed seventy others, and sent them in pairs ahead of Him to every city and place where He Himself was going to come ... 'Whatever city you enter and they receive you, eat what is set before you; and heal those in it who are sick, and say to them, "The kingdom of God has come near to you."'" Luke 10:1, 8-9*

With the Master at hand, these days were a steep learning curve for the disciples. *"I brought [my son] to your disciples, and they could not cure him,"* (Matthew 17:16) a desperate father once told Jesus.

Jesus immediately delivered the boy and the occasion quickly became a training exercise, not just for them but for every other disciple who still reads ...

> *"The disciples came to Jesus privately and said, 'Why*

could we not drive it out?' And He said to them, 'Because of the littleness of your faith; for truly I say to you, if you have faith the size of a mustard seed, you will say to this mountain, "Move from here to there," and it will move; and nothing will be impossible to you. But this kind does not go out except by prayer and fasting.'" Matthew 17:19-21

Jesus preached the gospel with signs following in order to confirm the message He preached, as a declaration to the multitudes that the kingdom of God was now here. In so doing, He modelled for His disciples the simple pattern they were to follow after His departure: preach the Gospel with signs following.

Jesus did not perform signs so that one day evangelicals would read out the miracles with preaching following. No! The pattern that Jesus modelled was one of preaching with signs following.

Disciples make mistakes - this is inferred in the word 'disciple'. A disciple, by definition, is a learner. And Jesus came to train them. So we have the likes of an apparently botched deliverance attempt where Jesus steps in and makes it His platform to teach on the importance of faith and of prayer.

Jesus came not only to reveal God and redeem man, but to reproduce His ministry in the disciples He would raise up over a three-year ministry training course.

To embrace all of Christ is not just to worship Him as God and receive Him as Saviour, but to follow Him as Example; to share His relationship of son-ship, His character of servanthood and His ministry of power.

Jesus came to model, teach and replicate in His disciples each of these areas of discipleship as a man empowered by the Holy Spirit. And it is by the same Holy Spirit that His disciples are adopted as sons, sanctified as instruments and anointed for service.

Like a golden thread through Luke's gospel, Jesus demonstrates and teaches how to be filled with the Holy Spirit. He prepares His disciples for the day when, like Elisha picking up the mantle of Elijah, they will carry the same anointing as He.

Jesus is introduced as the One who will baptise His disciples with the Holy Spirit ...

> *"John answered and said to them all, 'As for me, I baptise you with water; but One is coming who is mightier than I, and I am not fit to untie the thong of His sandals; He will baptise you with the Holy Spirit and fire.'"*
> Luke 3:16

Soon, Jesus is teaching His disciples how to receive the Holy Spirit ...

> *"'So I say to you, ask, and it will be given to you; seek, and you will find; knock, and it will be opened to you. For everyone who asks, receives; and he who seeks, finds; and to him who knocks, it will be opened. Now suppose one of you fathers is asked by his son for a fish; he will not give him a snake instead of a fish, will he? Or if he is asked for an egg, he will not give him a scorpion, will he? If you then, being evil, know how to give good gifts to your children, how much more will your heavenly Father give the Holy Spirit to those who ask Him?'"* Luke 11:9-13

Finally, Jesus instructs His disciples to wait for the power of the Spirit before their ministry can begin ...

> *"'And behold, I am sending forth the promise of My*

Father upon you; but you are to stay in the city until you are clothed with power from on high.'" Luke 24:49

After His ascension to heaven - 'mission control' - He would continue the work through the same Holy Spirit Who had empowered His own earthly ministry.

Just as the sons of the prophets had long ago observed Elisha take up the cloak of his master, and declared, *"The spirit of Elijah rests on Elisha,"* (II Kings 2:15) a day would soon come when the Jewish rulers, having blindly supposed the world to be now free of Jesus, would look upon Peter and John and *"recognise them as having been with Jesus."* (Acts 4:13)

When we speak of 'All of Christ', we acknowledge that in Him is found the full package of everything anyone could possibly need to see of the fullness of Deity: the revelation of God, the redemption of creation, and the raising up of a body on earth through which His fullness would continue to be made known after His return to the Father.

By seeing who Jesus is and what He came to do, we begin to see The Big Picture, a vision that begins with the Person of Christ in His coming, and continues today with Christ in His ascended place as *"head over all things to the church."* (Ephesians 1:22)

All of Christ in All the Church ...

PART II: ALL THE CHURCH

6. RUNNING THE CHURCH

"... And He put all things in subjection under His feet, and gave Him as head over all things to the church, which is His body, the fullness of Him who fills all in all."

Ephesians 1:22-23

C hrist became a man to reveal God, redeem mankind and raise disciples. Now it was time for Stage Two.

Christ was far from finished on earth; He had simply 'moved upstairs'! There was still the matter of a church to run. He has been doing this remotely, by the agency of the Holy Spirit, for 2,000 years.

Christ's death and resurrection are not the be-all-and-end-all; only together with the ascension do they become the beginning-of-all for the church.

Jesus did not *retire* to heaven. Rather, He ascended there to take up His executive role as head over all things to the church, seated at the right hand of the Father. He has been directing His body from there ever since, through the guidance and empowerment of God Immanent, the Holy Spirit.

This was the next phase Jesus had spoken of to Peter when he said, using the future continuous tense, "... I shall be building My church." (Matthew 16:18) The same Jesus who, for 2,000 years now, has been preparing "a place" for His disciples in heaven, has also been building a house for Himself on earth ... "... a dwelling of God in the Spirit." (Ephesians 2:22)

But as the apostle Paul taught so powerfully, Jesus is not just over the church - He is in it. He is the church's preeminent part, the Head. In fact, Paul so thoroughly associated Jesus with the church that he identified it as Christ's body.

Howard Snyder (2004, The Community of the King) expresses Paul's revelation wonderfully when he writes, "The church is nothing less than the body of no one less than Jesus Christ."

This was possibly the first spiritual lesson Paul learned on his conversion, when He was surely broken by these words, spoken directly from the mouth of Jesus: "Saul, Saul, why are you persecuting Me?" (Acts 9:4)

Implicit in Jesus' question, and foundational to Paul's revelation, was the understanding that what you do to the church, you do to Jesus. If you stone Stephen, you once more crucify Christ. To touch Jesus' disciples is to touch Him.

Paul described how Christ loves His church with the kind of love that the closest of human relationships, marriage, ought to emulate: "... Husbands ought to love their own wives as their own bodies." (Ephesians 5:28) Christ, Paul teaches, loves the church as His own body.

Jesus' personal identity is forever tied up in His church. As He will one day make clear at the great Judgement of the Nations

(Matthew 25:31-46), whatever has been done to the least of His own, is as good as done to Him.

After Jesus' death, resurrection and ascension, His very own ministry was reincarnated and multiplied through His body on earth, the church. It was to this end that He had promised to ask the Father to send the Holy Spirit, Another-of-the-same as Himself.

Paul's teaching on the church is revolutionary: just as the full-ness of the Godhead dwells bodily in Christ, so also the fullness of Christ is embodied in the church through the Third Person of the Trinity, the Holy Spirit.

In Colossians, we read ...

> "... In [Christ] all the fullness of Deity dwells in bodily form." (2:9)

... And in Colossians' 'twin epistle', Ephesians ...

> "[The church] is His body, the fullness of Him who fills all in all." (1:23)

Until we grasp the revelation of what the church of Jesus Christ truly is, we cannot begin to comprehend the big picture of God's plan for everything else.

So where better to begin our understanding of the body than with the Head Himself?

What roles does Jesus actually fulfil as head of the church?

Jesus Represents the Church

> "... Christ Jesus is He who died, yes, rather who was

> raised, who is at the right hand of God, who also inter-
> cedes for us." Romans 8:34

How aware are Christians that there is Someone in heaven interceding for us right now?

"There is one mediator between God and men, the man Jesus Christ," (I Timothy 2:5) Paul wrote elsewhere to Timothy.

One of Jesus' roles as head of the church is to represent us continually before the Father in heaven.

Jesus' presence at God's right hand is a permanent statement of
the once-for-all work He accomplished on our behalf through
the cross - the place where He sat down after His labours.

But His position is also the locus of His ongoing advocacy, as He
leads us towards the completion of the work now begun ...

> *"... I am confident of this very thing, that He who
> began a good work in you will perfect it until the day
> of Jesus Christ."* Philippians 1:6

I wonder what things Jesus might be interceding for us, whether
individually or collectively, as He represents us before the
Father? Are they likely to be much different from the interces-
sions He made on His disciples' behalf while here on earth?

Our deliverance from evil? ...

> *"I do not ask You to take them out of the world, but to
> keep them from the evil one."* John 17:15

Our sanctification in the truth? ...

> *"Sanctify them in the truth; Your word is truth."* John

17:17

Our unity in Him that the world might see? ...

> *"... That they may all be one; even as You, Father, are in Me and I in You, that they also may be in Us, so that the world may believe that You sent Me."* John 17:21

Could Jesus be praying such things on our behalf today?

Have you ever considered that the final, glorious outcome of our salvation will be the fruit, not of our best efforts, but of Jesus' prayer life?

If not, perhaps we should stop right now and give thanks to the *"High Priest of our confession,"* (Hebrews 3:1) the one who *"ever lives to make intercession for us"* (Hebrews 7:25)!

Have there ever been moments when, driving along the road or going about your work, you have felt an inner consciousness that someone, somewhere is praying for you?

The good news is that the child of God doesn't have to *feel* this - we simply need to believe the Scriptures.Someone very special indeed, not just anyone, is continuously bringing us before the Father in heaven.

If that doesn't produce a warm glow in the belly, then warm bellies aren't worth the value we afford them!

But what else, other than interceding, might Jesus be doing at the right hand of the Father?

Jesus Resources the Church

> *"When He ascended on high ... He gave gifts to men."*

Ephesians 4:8

The Holy Spirit is both the Gift and the Gift-Bearer. And it was from the place of His ascension to the Father's side that the Gift and His gifts have been poured out, to empower and resource the church ...

> "... He who believes in Me, the works that I do, he will do also; and greater works than these he will do; **because I go to the Father**." John 7:38-39 (Emphasis mine)

Jesus had promised that, after he was glorified, His disciples would receive the Holy Spirit. This is what happened in Acts chapter 2.

Jesus asked the Father to send the Holy Spirit upon the church. The answer was delivered ten days after His ascension, on the Day of Pentecost, with around 120 believers "... *all together in one place.*" (Acts 2:1)

The upper room in Jerusalem was the place where God's collective, the church, was empowered for ministry, just as Jesus Himself had been on the occasion of His baptism in the River Jordan.

By the Spirit's presence and anointing, the church was equipped to be a complete expression of Jesus' Person and ministry on earth.

The Holy Spirit is the Other Helper whose impact is identical to that of Jesus. His outpouring ushered in a new age where Jesus' followers were no longer excluded by physical distance from direct, immediate and personal access to both Jesus and the Father.

The sending of the Spirit, released by Jesus' ascension, brought about the biblical *"last days"* (Acts 2:17); the age of the New Testament church on earth; the time regarding which Jesus Himself had said, *"It is to your advantage that I go away"* (John 16:7); the period in which we still live today.

By sending the same Holy Spirit who anointed Jesus, the Father equipped the church with all the gifts and graces that accompanied Jesus' own earthly ministry. The disciples were now not just delegates *of* Jesus, but delegates *like* Jesus.

This became immediately evident from Pentecost onwards. Such was the spiritual power that came upon these first believers that, when Peter stood up to declare what was taking place and 'pull in the net' with a bold command to repent, 3,000 souls were added to their number in just one day.

There is surely no way that, among that great number in Jerusalem, there were not many who, only a few weeks before, had been among the crowd that cried *"Crucify Him!"* One thing is certain: very few, if any, of these converts could have been first-time hearers about Jesus.

So what could be the explanation for this great display of repentance, the great turn-around, now underway? Nothing other than the power of the Holy Spirit upon the church - the same anointing that had been upon Jesus Himself.

Then in the next chapter, Peter squares eyes on a lame beggar outside the temple and, with bold, unquestioning faith, tells him, *"Look at us!"* (Acts 3:4)

"Look at us!"?

Should he not have been urging, *'Look to **Jesus**!'*?

But how could he, when Jesus wasn't here anymore?

From now on, to look at Peter and John was to look at Jesus still at work. Not because they had replaced Jesus, but because Jesus, by the Holy Spirit, had now invested Himself in them.

To look at Christ's body functioning in the fullness of the Holy Spirit is to see Jesus.

The result for the lame beggar in Acts chapter 3 was the same as for anyone healed in the Gospels, as he danced into the temple praising God.

If the scribes and Pharisees thought the crucixion of Jesus meant they could now get back to life as normal, 'pre-Jesus', they had another think coming! Jesus didn't leave to disappear; He left to multiply!

The story of 'God and sons' was just getting going!

In the next chapter again, the Jewish rulers were amazed to observe the Jesus they thought they had got rid of, His anointing now embedded in Peter and John, as they *"recognised them as having been with Jesus."* (Acts 4:13)

These first disciples ought to have been beaten down by the sight of their leader's life extinguished, and under the fear of the certainty of a similar fate falling upon them should they decide to follow His example.

Yes, they had been broken by Christ crucified; but now they were empowered by Christ ascended. The same Spirit that had been upon Him was now transferred to them, emboldening them as fearless, joyful martyrs, just like Jesus.

The Greek *martures* is translated "witnesses" in the New Testament ...

> *"... You will receive power when the Holy Spirit has come upon you; and you shall be My witnesses ..."* Acts 1:8

But the outpouring of the Holy Spirit was about so much more than even the power to be witnesses.

The Full Package of Jesus' Ministry

All the gifts and graces that attended Jesus' earthly ministry, Stage 1, would now, by the Holy Spirit, attend His earthly ministry, Stage 2, through the church operating under His headship.

Jesus, the ascended Apostle and Prophet, would give apostles and prophets to the church in order to deliver His continued apostolic and prophetic expression through the whole of His body.

This is as good a point as any to address a matter of confusion that, for some, is a major obstacle to the big picture in God's plan for everything.

Cessationism

There is no biblical basis for a doctrine of so called 'cessationism', the idea that the supernatural gifts of the Holy Spirit, as evident through the ministry of the early church, were at some point recalled to heaven, a kind of 'Retro-Pentecost' event. Such a significant day should surely have merited warning somewhere in either the Old or New Testaments. But not a hint of it.

Paul did say to the Corinthians that gifts such as speaking in tongues and prophesying would one day be done away; but that day, he wrote, would be *"when the perfect comes."* (I Corinthians 13:9-10)

Cessationism, clutching at straws, perhaps panicked at the idea of the church being washed away in a river beyond human control, has suggested that the completion of the New Testament canonical scriptures represented the 'coming of the perfect'; the idea being that, now that we have the Bible, we no longer need the gifts of the Spirit.

Think that through.

Jesus Himself, 'the Word made flesh', accepted the confirmation of His message by signs and wonders. But today's believers? No, we're above that - we don't need such things because we have His words in print!

Is it not arrogance to think that both Jesus and the first apostles required something we have somehow matured beyond; that our modern-day world is so advanced and spiritually minded that such gifts are no longer needed?

The Book of Acts, overflowing with signs and wonders, is not the 'Magic Faraway Tree' of a long-gone church; it is the prototype of a historic, missional movement, its spiritual resources as necessary for the completion of the task as for its commencement.

Apostles and Prophets Today

Cessationism is nowhere more strongly asserted than in the rejection of the ministry of apostles and prophets today. There is, of course, an understandable fear of self-appointed messianic figures, with cult followings, making supposedly infallible additions and amendments to the Scriptures, and leading gullible Christians over the precipice of destruction.

But was this not also a danger in the first century world of Peter, John and Paul, when false apostles were also a feature? And why should modern-day apostles be any more likely to be marked by megalomania or messianic complexes than the genuine apostolic ministries of the first century?

People who reject apostles and prophets today probably do so for a lack of understanding of what Ephesians 4 apostles and prophets actually are.

There is clearly an irreplaceable role for *"the twelve apostles of the Lamb"* (Revelation 21:14) who knew Jesus in the flesh, whose number will obviously never be added to. But what of the many gifts of apostleship poured out *"after"* Jesus had ascended on high (Ephesians 4:7, 11)? What about the string of apostles mentioned by name in the New Testament, not least Paul who wasn't even a believer during Jesus' earthly ministry?

To understand the gift of apostle, we need to understand the pure meaning of the word. An *apostolos* (Greek) simply means 'a sent one', an ambassador who crosses regions to represent a sending ruler. An apostle is a servant who represents only the interests of his kingdom and never his own; authorised and re-sourced to represent the realm from which he came - does this not sound like Jesus' description of Himself in John's Gospel?

Apostle Jesus came to earth, sent by the Father to represent His kingdom and preach His message of reconciliation. After Jesus' ascension, the first apostles were sent out into 'regions beyond', on an apostolic mission to extend this same message.

The apostle Peter crossed enormous cultural and institutional boundaries, and at great reputational risk among his Jewish brethren, to deliver the kingdom of God, in the power of the Holy Spirit, to a Roman centurion's household in Acts chapter 10.

Randomly jump forward seventeen centuries and more than 2,000 miles to England, and we find pioneers like John Wesley, one of the more famed apostles of history. The man is pelted by the missiles and insults of his detractors – just like Paul, they called him the *"scum"* of his day (I Corinthians 4:13) – as he breaks through the taboos and ecclesiastical boundaries of es-tablished religion to ignite the movement of the moment: Meth-odism. Scan through church history and apostles, just as in the

Book of Acts, are everywhere to be found.

The Christian story is punctuated by the ministries of apostles and prophets, great and small, a few Wesleys, but many buried without record, simply demonstrating that the Christ who ascended to build His church never did 'up tools'.

The term 'first generation church' is a misnomer. Biblically, the church of Jesus Christ is only one generation. God has no 'grandchildren'. As Peter wrote to far-scattered believers of his time, the church is *"... a chosen generation."* (I Peter 2:9) The idea that church history can be divided into different ages, with God's children in one period inheriting resources not available to siblings at another time, for exactly the same task, has no biblical basis whatsoever.

The *"last days"* of Scripture began with the empowerment of the church at Pentecost (Acts 2:17) and, given that the end has still not come, we remain in the same dispensation today. (We will return to this in Section 3.)

What a relief that the ascended Jesus who launched Operation Church 2,000 years ago is still directing The Mission today, and that His gifts and tools have never become obsolete! And basic to His strategy of keeping His church mobilised on its apostolic mission is the continued provision to His church of apostles. This ought not to require stating, but given the foundational nature of these gifts we should not be surprised to see them challenged.

Where are today's apostolic movements?

Perhaps this question is best answered by other questions. Where is the church breaking into new areas, often amidst great difficulty and hostility, planting new churches, making disciples and raising up indigenous leaders in great numbers? Where is radical change being inspired and mobilised in ways most unsettling to institutional orthodoxy – orders that have most to lose by God 'taking over' – yet doing so with godliness, grace and humility and without compromising biblical truth? Who are the ones continually faced with character assassination by those (in religious or secular power) who feel threatened?

Such is the portion of apostles, despised as the "scum" and "dregs" of Paul's day (I Corinthians 4:13), and maligned ever since! Frequently revered after they're gone, but despised while alive. They are the ground-breakers who call the church back to its apostolic DNA. They understand the contract they signed up to, take hostility on the chin and forgive where wronged – after all, is that not what they also did to Jesus before they received mercy themselves? As with apostles, so with prophets and every other gifting of the ascended Christ. These gifts will attract the same response to Jesus' disciples as they did to Jesus Himself.

Apostles and prophets need to be singled out because they have been subjected to a degree of rejection not experienced by the other three gifts mentioned in Ephesians chapter 4. It is not hard to see why. If these gifts are as fundamental to a functioning church as Ephesians declares them to be, then it would clearly be an intelligent strategy of the 'gates of hell' to marginalise them and, thereby, undermine the church at base.

Those who reject these ministries today take scriptural texts such as Ephesians 2:20, which talks of the church having been "built on the foundation of the apostles and prophets," and neatly identify the 'apostles' as the books of the New Testament and 'prophets' as the books of the Old. This fanciful approach to biblical interpretation not only overlooks prophets in the New Testament, such as Judas and Silas (Acts 15) and Agabus (Acts 21), but is also out of context with Paul's teaching later in the same epistle, where he integrates apostles and prophets with a fuller list of 'fivefold ministries', as keys to a healthily maturing body.

Since we now have the canon of the Old and New Testaments, cessationist thinking goes, we no longer need apostles and prophets. But if that is the case, then why not make the same application to evangelists, pastors and teachers? Jesus the Apostle and Prophet needs to be known today as much as Jesus the Good Shepherd, and He is to be known as such only through His body, which He Himself has graced with these gifts.

Equipping the Church

> *"And He [the ascended Christ] gave some as apostles, and some as prophets, and some as evangelists, and some as pastors and teachers, for the equipping of the saints for the work of service, to the building up of the body of Christ ..."* Ephesians 4:11-12

This is why Jesus resources the church with the leadership gifts of apostles, prophets, evangelists, pastors and teachers: so that the full package of every aspect of Christ's ministry might be expressed through the entirety of the church through which His headship is to be expressed. This is such a crucial key to the big picture of *'all of Christ in all the church.'*

The measure of the presence of any of these leadership gifts in the church is the extent to which these dimensions are evident in the culture of entire church. The measure of an ascension gift of evangelist is not a charismatic personality, an eloquent speaker, or even extraordinary drawing power; rather, it is the extent to which the people around the evangelist become more evangelistic themselves. The evangelist, like all the other ministries, according to Ephesians chapter 4, is given to equip the whole church to express Evangelist Jesus.

Jesus the Evangelist resources His body with evangelists so that the church might be ignited in soulwinning. The same holds true of pastors and teachers whose role, by their faithful example, is not to do all the work, but to develop a church culture where the whole family becomes more nurturing and caring, learning to effectively raise others in the faith.

Jesus ascended to resource the whole church to represent the fullness of His ministry; a church serviced, equipped and matured by leaders whose giftings, imparted and developed by the Holy Spirit, become the conduit through which the kingdom of heaven comes to earth in the church.

Jesus ascended to heaven to represent the church and to resource the church. And, as *"head over all things to the church,"* He ascended to run the church.

Jesus Runs the Church

Matthew's Gospel has been referred to as 'The Gospel of the Church' simply because it is the only one of the four where Jesus uses the term *ekklesia*, translated 'church'.

On each of the two occasions 'church' is used, Jesus immediately goes on to speak of the power of 'binding and loosing' which would be delegated to His body on earth.

> *"I also say to you that you are Peter, and upon this rock I will build My church* [ekklesia]*; and the gates of Hades will not overpower it. I will give you the keys of the kingdom of heaven; and whatever you bind on earth shall have been bound in heaven, and whatever you loose on earth shall have been loosed in heaven."* Matthew 16:18-19

> *"If he (your sinning brother) refuses to listen to them (those who challenge him), tell it to the church* [ekkle-

> sia]; *and if he refuses to listen even to the church* [ekklesia], *let him be to you as a Gentile and a tax collector. I say to you, whatever you bind on earth shall have been bound in heaven; and whatever you loose on earth shall have been loosed in heaven."* Matthew 18:17-18

Much has been said and written about binding and loosing, but the bottom line is that Jesus was authorising the church to govern in His physical absence, yet from a place of direct spiritual connection to, and delegation from, Him in heaven.

While the New Living Translation helpfully translates 'binding and loosing' as 'forbidding and permitting', thus conveying the essential idea of the church's authority to govern, the same translation (along with the King James Version and various others) unfortunately misses the tenses used, reading simply: *"Whatever you forbid (bind) on earth will be forbidden (bound) in heaven, and whatever you permit (loose) on earth will be permitted (loosed) in heaven."*

But that's not exactly what Jesus said!

Note the Greek tenses in the record of what Jesus actually said: *"Whatever you forbid on earth* **will have been** *forbidden in heaven, and whatever you permit on earth* **will have been** *permitted in heaven."* (Emphasis mine)

This may seem like splitting hairs, but it is relevant to the revelation of an ascended Jesus now building His church from heaven. The underpinning truth that some translations could have done more to clarify is that the 'forbidding and permitting' happen in heaven *before* they happen on earth.

The church does not carry arbitrary authority to act independently of Jesus, and no believer should expect the Holy Spirit simply to step in and back up anything he or she decides to say or do.

Only those who are *under* authority *have* authority.

This, as we have seen so clearly, was the example of Jesus' own earthly ministry as He repeatedly emphasised that He did nothing of His own initiative, only saying and doing that which He first heard and saw the Father saying and doing.

When Jesus said, *"I shall be building My church,"* He clearly had in mind an ongoing down-flow of divine wisdom and understanding, by which He intended to run the church from His throne in heaven. It was precisely for this that the Holy Spirit was to be sent.

And so we see a very significant example of binding and loosing in Acts chapter 15, where the apostles and elders passed an enormously liberating ruling to the Gentile believers in Syria and Cilicia with the words, *"It seemed good to the Holy Spirit and to us ..."* (Acts 15:28)

As the church rapidly grew among the Gentiles, a ruling was required for which there was no specific Old Testament text, as to whether the new converts should be required to be circumcised. The Jerusalem council ruling effectively rescued the Gentiles from the dangerous pressures of some to come under Moses in order to access Jesus. Interestingly, the primary lead in the Council's decision was Peter, the one to whom Jesus had originally said, *"Whatever you bind/loose on earth will have been bound/loosed in heaven."*

The Acts 15 ruling is one of the most obvious and prominent examples of binding and loosing, but the story of the New Testament church is brimming over with examples, whether great governmental directives such as these, or numerous smaller, localised instances of church leaderships and individual believers apprehending and releasing the solutions of heaven on earth.

The point is that the ascended Christ is running His church on earth through believers who are so connected to Him by the Holy Spirit that the apostle Paul was moved to declare to the Ephesians, not only that we have been made *"His body"* (1:23), but that we have been *"seated ... with Him in the heavenly places in Christ Jesus."* (2:6)

As He is here on earth with us by His Spirit, so we are here with Him in heaven (yes, heaven is 'here' to us); as members of Christ's body, we are citizens of Heaven, right now. It is in this inseparable, one body relationship that the church is run on earth by its ascended head, Jesus Christ.

The Kingdom of God in the Holy Spirit

We cannot understand the church in any depth without speaking of the kingdom of God.

The kingdom of God is about the Lordship or reign of God in Jesus Christ. The church is not the kingdom of God, but it is the agency, or embassy, through which the kingdom of God is preached, demonstrated and represented on earth. The church is none other than God's ambassadorial people on earth.

It is in order that the kingdom of God come on earth that the church has been given the Holy Spirit, for there is no other means on earth through which the kingdom of God is able to come than through the personal presence of the Holy Spirit.

Paul wrote that *"the kingdom of God is ... righteousness and peace and joy **in the Holy Spirit**."* (Romans 14:17, emphasis mine) Yes, the kingdom of God is about righteousness and peace and joy, but these virtues are but fruits of the personal presence of the Holy Spirit. When we have Him, we automatically have them ... and with them is the kingdom reign of God.

Notice Jesus' response to His disciples before His ascension to heaven, when they asked Him if this was when He was going to restore *"the kingdom"* to Israel. His response was immediate:

> *"It is not for you to know times or epochs which the Father has fixed by His own authority; but you will receive power when the Holy Spirit has come upon you ..."* Acts 1:7-8

The disciples were, of course, thinking about the earthly reign of King Jesus, a future age which, according to the end of The Book, He will one day return to establish.

But Jesus' attention was now upon the age of the church, *His* church, the body through which the *'powers of the age to come'* should be demonstrated in advance on earth; a Gospel-preaching, Kingdom-heralding people through which the nations of the earth should be occupied under His ambassadorial authority.

When the Holy Spirit was poured out on the Day of Pentecost, God was doing more than resourcing the church with spiritual gifts; He was establishing the kingdom reign of Jesus Christ in the hearts and lives, lifestyles and communities of His people.

For the kingdom of God is *"in the Holy Spirit."* And when the church, or any believer, has been filled with the Holy Spirit, they are directed, inspired and empowered to bind on earth what has been bound in heaven, and to loose on earth what has been loosed in heaven, simply by living under the authority of Christ in the fullness of the Holy Spirit.

I have come to believe that the primary cause of resistance to the fullness of the Holy Spirit is resistance to the Lordship, or mastery, of Jesus Christ. Those who resist the Holy Spirit are often those who wish to remain in charge of their own lives.

It is no coincidence that in Luke's Gospel (chapter 11), when Jesus begins the Lord's Prayer with *"Thy kingdom come, Thy will be done,"* he goes straight on to teach about asking to be filled with the Holy Spirit.

For a disciple to be filled with the Holy Spirit is effectively for the ascended Jesus Himself to emphatically declare,

> *I am in charge of this child's life. My kingdom has now occupied his heart and presides over his will. He no longer speaks from himself, but from Me. Because I am his source, what he says is what he knows Me to be saying, just as what I have said came not from Me, but from My Father.*
>
> *When he proclaims forgiveness to repentant sinners, it is not his offer he extends but Mine. When he touches broken bodies and shattered lives with My compassion, the ones he touches are healed inasmuch as they are the ones I have been moved to touch. When he speaks what he has heard Me speak in the darkness, My word will lighten up the most desperate place and bring life, hope and a future.*
>
> *And when My kingdom people come together under the reign of My Spirit and My word, the things they bind and forbid on earth will have been bound and forbidden heaven, and the things they loose and permit on earth will have been loosed and permitted in heaven.*

These are among the marvellous things Jesus has been doing for 2,000 years since His ascension to the right hand of the Father: representing, resourcing and running the church, His body on earth.

Just as the fullness of God is revealed in the person of Jesus, so the fullness of Jesus is revealed in the collective of His people: one body, which He has created, is multiplying and maturing until finally, one day, at the *"summing up of all things in Christ"* (Ephesians 1:10), it will add up to a full revelation of Christ Himself.

This is the big picture of Paul's letter to the Ephesians:

All of Christ in all the Church.

7. THE HOLY SPIRIT

*"I will ask the Father, and He will give
you another Helper, so that He may
be with you forever; the Helper is the
Spirit of truth, whom the world cannot
receive, because it does not see Him or
know Him; but you know Him because
He remains with you and will be in you."*

John 14:16-17

W e have already seen how, when Jesus told the disciples to expect the Spirit as *"another"* Helper, He was speaking of One just like Himself, in the same way as He Himself is just like the Father.

Jesus was pointing ahead to a relationship with, and experience of, the Holy Spirit that they did not have during His earthly ministry. He had been *"with"* them but would be *"in"* them in a new way. In the same way as Jesus had walked in the power of the Spirit in the Gospels, His body, the church, would walk in the power of the Spirit in Acts.

Biblically, there is no such thing as a first-century, or early-fathers, dispensation. There is only the age of the church, defined in Acts 2:17 as *"the last days."*

The Last Days began at Pentecost and, given that Christ has yet to return, we remain in the Last Days today. This perhaps needs to be stressed because we still hear evangelical preachers say things like, *'We are living in the Last Days before Christ's return!'* as if this has not been the case for two millennia.

I'm far from suggesting it is unhealthy for Christians to believe theirs could be 'the *last* of the last days' - just ask any teacher or store manager if the knowledge that 'an inspection around the corner' doesn't promote vigilance and attention to practice! It's good to promote urgency and vigilance.

I am simply emphasising that, biblically, the 21st century church lives in a common dispensation with the first century apostles.

Same age.

Same mission.

Same resources.

This is the age when Christ is building on earth a human dwelling place described by Paul as *"a dwelling of God in the Spirit."* (Ephesians 2:22)

The same Jesus who ascended to prepare a place for us in heaven has been simultaneously building for Himself a temple on earth. To use Peter's words, *"... You also, as living stones, are being built up as a spiritual house ..."* (I Peter 2:5)

How has He been doing this? Quite simply through the personal presence of the Holy Spirit, the omnipresent One who is *with us at the same time as being with Christ.* The fastest internal speed in the world cannot match the One who is already here while simultaneously in unbroken communion with the Father and the Son!

I think it would be good to pause here and give due honour to the personal presence of the Holy Spirit.

God Immanent: The Holy Spirit

Just as we cannot know the Father without Jesus, so we cannot know Jesus or, by extension, the Father except through the Holy Spirit. I can think of no better explanation for Jesus describing blasphemy against the Holy Spirit as unforgiveable:

> *"Truly I say to you, all sins will be forgiven the sons*
> *and daughters of men, and whatever blasphemies they*
> *commit; but whoever blasphemes against the Holy*
> *Spirit never has forgiveness, but is guilty of an eternal*
> *sin."* Mark 3:28-29

How can we possibly be saved if we reject the only One able to lead us into salvation?

The Father and the Son are in Heaven. They are not personally here on earth. It is the Holy Spirit, 'God Immanent', who is actually here, and through whom alone we are able to have any meaningful connection with Christ and the Father.

There used to be an almost heretical idea floating around, and it may still linger, perhaps through the sometimes misleading effect of Old English King James-speak, that the Holy Spirit does not talk about Himself and, therefore, neither should we talk about - much less to - Holy Spirit!

This insultingly misguided notion was once justified by Jesus' teaching that, when the Spirit came, He would *"not speak of Himself."* (John 16:13, KJV, emphasis mine) Both the context within which Jesus was speaking and the Greek from which 17th century Englishmen were translating, are plain that the word *'of'*, in today's language, should be understood as *'from'* rather than *'about'*.

Jesus was not saying that the Holy Spirit would not speak *about*

Himself, but that He would not speak *from* Himself; that is, He would not speak from His own independent source.

This was the same Jesus who had made it repeatedly clear that He Himself spoke nothing of His own initiative, but only out of that spoken to Him by the Father. Now He was saying that, when the Holy Spirit came, He would be just like Him, not speaking out of His own initiative, but from the one source of the Triune God.

To say that we should neither speak to the Holy Spirit nor expect the Spirit to speak about Himself, is the ridiculous equivalent to saying that, during His earthly ministry, no one should have spoken to Jesus or asked Him to speak about Himself.

Visiting Glasgow a number of years ago, the late Canadian preacher, Ern Baxter, asked his audience to imagine the scene in heaven on Christ's ascension. Baxter's method may sound irreverent to some, but if I still remember it 40 years later, his use of humour was clearly effective!

This is how Baxter put it ...

> *"Imagine Jesus ascending to heaven and sitting down at the right hand of the Father, and then Father and Son, turning their eyes to the Holy Spirit, say, 'Now it's Your turn!' ...*

How might *you* feel if you were the Holy Spirit? ...

> *"If I were the Holy Spirit, I'd say, 'What?! ... After what they did to Him?! ...'"*

That was where Baxter's humour ended as he launched into full passionate flow ...

105

"I do not want to take anything away from what our precious Lord Jesus went through for us for three whole years, climaxing in the horror of Gethsemane and Golgotha. But friends, what Jesus went through for three years, our precious Holy Spirit has been subjected to for two thousand. He too has been despised and rejected. He has been grieved and quenched in the church. Just like Jesus, He has been called Satan by religious people. Perhaps almost as bad, He has been depersonalised, even referred to as 'It' by people who have Him in their life, unconsciously defining Him as a force rather than the Third Person of the Trinity ..."

As I reflect on these words, I am convicted of the times I have 'talked past' the Holy Spirit in the room, referring to Him in the third person as if He weren't present, as if he couldn't hear my thoughts and speak to me directly. Were I constantly to refer to another human being in the same room as 'he' or 'she', but never 'you', as if they weren't even present, always excluded from the conversation, I should rightly be considered rude. The ignored one might reasonably think, *'Does this person even want me here?'*

Maybe we should pray right now? ...

Forgive me, Holy Spirit. I realise You are here, by the grace of God, to work in my life; to open the Scriptures to me, making Jesus real to me, and revealing what Jesus has done for me by Your power; to work what the Father has sent You to do in me; to direct, correct and encourage me; to convict me of need, transform my thought-life and empower me for service; to change me continually into the likeness of Jesus Christ; to equip me in making Jesus known to others, just as others, only because of Your help, have made Him known to me.

Thank God for the precious Holy Spirit, the One in whom alone we know the presence of God and through whom alone our ascended Saviour runs His church!

We will go on to look at the gifts of the Spirit by which Christ operates His church, but all the gifts of the Spirit must take their place only after giving due place to the greatest Gift of all; the Gift which *is* the Holy Spirit Himself.

He, the Person of the Holy Spirit, is the Promise. What He *does* is wonderful but before and above all He does, we must embrace and worship Him for who He *is.*

Yes, He opens blind eyes, but He also struck with blindness both Saul of Tarsus and Elymas the magician, each for a time. Yes, He raises the dead, but lying to the Holy Spirit also sent Ananias and Sapphira to a sudden, early grave!

If I put the gift before the Giver, healing before the Healer, there are truths about who He is that I will miss, maybe even blank out, as I start 'talking past Him' in the room again.

Expecting Him to 'remain in the room' on *our* terms is something none of us should presume upon. The Holy Spirit through whom Christ runs His church only run the church on His own terms.

It is so crucial that we put the Person of the Holy Spirit, which begins experientially with our baptism in Him, ahead of the gifts He brings to us, and before the works he goes on to do through us. This is something the late David Pawson was keen to emphasise. Kindly reviewing a small book I wrote on the baptism in the Holy Spirit, Pawson sent me this observation ...

> *"... Some have tried to promote the charismatic gifts by dropping the teaching of the baptism in the Holy Spirit, but the gifts will quickly disappear without the*

baptism."

The empowerment and the gifts of the Spirit come on His own terms, and so it all must start in our relationship with the Spirit Himself. It is the personal influence of the Holy Spirit in our lives through which alone Christ's kingdom reign comes to be expressed.

Pawson's letter went on to emphasise two main purposes of the baptism in the Holy Spirit ...

> *"I have always taught the baptism's object is twofold:* ***purity for self*** *and* ***power for others****, both being essential for witness."*

Purity for self

Have you ever considered that the Holy Spirit is the only member of the Trinity whose name is modified by an adjective?

Holy!

Among the very first attributes and influences of the Holy Spirit in our lives is with regard to personal sin and righteousness.

This is the way Jesus said it would be ...

> *"He, when He comes, will convict the world regarding sin, and righteousness, and judgment ..."* John 16:8

I will never forget the afternoon in 1982 in a Glasgow University student hall of residence when a knock came to my door. Not long a Christian myself, I opened the door to a friend from my far-from-Jesus days who simply looked at me and said, *"I want to change."*

That evening, I had the privilege of joining Andrew in prayer as he asked Jesus Christ to be his Saviour, and it is a wonderful thing that he, and now his grown family, still love and serve the Lord today.

But what happened to bring him to this point?

He had been speaking unfairly and unkindly about another friend of both of us, who happened to be a follower of Jesus. Troubled by guilt, Andrew eventually went to him to apologise for his behaviour.

Much to Andrew's amazement, this young man knew about it and, being a Christian, had already forgiven him. This only added to his feeling of guilt, to use a Bible term, *"heaping hot coals upon his head."* (Romans 12:20)

The Holy Spirit was using the witness of our friend to convict Andrew not just of his wrongdoing on this occasion, but of his general sinful state; bringing him to the only One who could bring him to forgiveness and relieve his guilty conscience.

This is the work of the Holy Spirit. Repentance is essential to salvation, but it can only happen through a stirred and awakened conscience. There cannot be repentance without felt need.

David's friend of 'hot coals', Paul, was actually the same young man whom God had used to bring me to salvation in the same residence eight months previously.

It was around 2am on Saturday morning, 6th February, 1982, when, drunken and dishevelled, this 18-year old student, much too young to be such a wreck, found himself - myself - outside on a cold, dark night, keys lost. Seeing a top floor light, I launched a fistful of pebbles up at the window.

The face that appeared belonged to Paul, at that time a backslidden Christian whose friend had only recently supplied me with cannabis. Paul let me into the building and, without any keys, the only room open to me was his.

We began to talk until, probably nearly 4am, Paul, to my astonishment, opened up and began to read a Bible. As he read, I became instantly conscious of the presence of a God who was holy and good - everything that I was not.

The fact that this God would even talk to me became the 'hot coals' that brought me to repentance. Tears streaming down my face, I repeated the only thing I knew to say at that moment: *"Forgive me, Jesus. Forgive me, Jesus. Forgive me, Jesus ..."*

Paul looked up and, in astonishment, asked, *"What's happening, Alistair?"*

In moments, he too was weeping his way back to Jesus, instantly conscious of what he himself had turned away from. The same Holy Spirit who would soon supply the power to reach Andrew, was first of all dealing with the matter of Paul's sinful heart.

Before power for others, purity for self.

These two 'P's, as Pawson pointed out, are the work of the same Holy Spirit. And they are not just for a moment of initiation, but for the whole journey of life on earth.

It would be nice to think my tears of repentance were over that night, but that was just the beginning!

The appeal of the Lord's Prayer, *"Give us **this day** ..."*, implies that everything contained in that prayer, not merely the daily bread, but also the *"forgive us our sins"* bit, is a daily need.

Nearly forty years after my first night of repentance, I sometimes find myself thinking, *"Dear Lord, should I not be sorted by now?!"*

Only last year, at a UK gathering of church leaders, after one fairly heated discussion, again the Holy Spirit had to deal with me, not letting me leave the room until, in the presence of all, I humbled myself, apologising unreservedly to a brother for disrespectful words and an inexcusable attitude.

He is the *Holy* Spirit. He will not tolerate sin in a disciple's life, and His presence will not allow us to enjoy inner peace without regular cleansing.

It's presumptuous to expect power for others without accepting purity for self. The Holy Spirit will faithfully remind us of this.

God forbid that the power of the Gospel should be undermined by our testimony.

Perhaps a major reason why so much of the church appears to lack so much power is because the Holy Spirit simply will not uncouple power from purity, as if they came from different sources?

The scriptural contexts for grieving and quenching the Holy Spirit should not be lost on Bible believers ...

> *"Let no unwholesome word come out of your mouth, but if there is any good word for edification according to the need of the moment, say that, so that it will give grace to those who hear. **Do not grieve the Holy Spirit of God**, by whom you were sealed for the day of redemption. All bitterness, wrath, anger, clamour, and slander must be removed from you, along with all malice. Be kind to one another, compassionate, forgiving each other, just as God in Christ also has forgiven you."*
> Ephesians 4: 29-32 (Emphasis mine)

> *"See that no one repays another with evil for evil, but*

always seek what is good for one another and for all people. Rejoice always, pray without ceasing, in everything give thanks; for this is the will of God for you in Christ Jesus. **Do not quench the Spirit***, do not despise prophetic utterances, but examine everything; hold firmly to that which is good, abstain from every form of evil."* I Thessalonians 5:15-22 (Emphasis mine)

The ministry of the Holy Spirit is to nurture and mature in Christ's body the holy nature and sound character of Jesus Himself; what we simply call Christ-likeness. The message of Christ, declared by a people who behave like Christ, is an unstoppable force.

Christ-like attitude and Godly living are the work of the Holy Spirit, every bit as much as extraordinary spiritual gifts. Together, they amount to the full package of the church's empowerment to *"go into all the world and preach the gospel to all creation."* (Mark 16:15)

Some Pentecostals have limited the Holy Spirit to power, while some evangelicals have confined Him to purity. The Bible, on the other hand, does not provide for such a dichotomy.

The full example of Christ, and of the first disciples, is one of both moral purity and spiritual power. It is not a matter of which we might prefer, but of what God has modelled in Christ, prescribed in His word and supplied by the Holy Spirit.

Power for others

Jesus was very clear with His disciples about the purpose of what would happen on the Day of Pentecost:

"… You will receive power when the Holy Spirit has come upon you; and you shall be My witnesses both in

*Jerusalem and in all Judea, and Samaria, and as far as
the remotest part of the earth."* Acts 1:8

Jesus Christ, through His substitutionary death and resurrection, had paid the price of redemption. It was now the task of those redeemed to make that redemption known to all mankind.

No small task. No small power required.

How disastrous it would have been, had Christ accomplished the greatest work of all history, but the story of it - much less benefit from it - never got out of town! What a tragic waste of priceless resource that would have been.

From the day I was born again, I had a longing in my heart to lead others to Jesus. The Jesus who had searched me out began to stir in me the need to reach others too. The need to see others born again is the inevitable outflow of a genuine encounter with Jesus Christ.

It is this longing that moves us as disciples to seek God for His power - not so that we might live in a self-satisfying bubble of heaven on earth, but that we might effectively make disciples for Christ. There is nothing like Pentecost to take us out of ourselves and propel us outward, to the world Christ died for.

This consciousness of need of others was at the heart Jesus' own teaching on seeking the Holy Spirit ...

> *"Then He said to them, 'Suppose one of you has a
> friend, and goes to him at midnight and says to him,
> "Friend, lend me three loaves; for a friend of mine has
> come to me from a journey, and I have nothing to set
> before him"; and from inside he answers and says, "Do
> not bother me; the door has already been shut and*

my children and I are in bed; I cannot get up and give
you anything." I tell you, even though he will not get
up and give him anything because he is his friend, yet
because of his persistence he will get up and give him
as much as he needs.

"'So I say to you, ask, and it will be given to you; seek,
and you will find; knock, and it will be opened to you.
For everyone who asks, receives; and he who seeks,
finds; and to him who knocks, it will be opened. Now
suppose one of you fathers is asked by his son for a
fish; he will not give him a snake instead of a fish, will
he? Or if he is asked for an egg, he will not give him a
scorpion, will he? If you then, being evil, know how to
give good gifts to your children, how much more will
your heavenly Father give the Holy Spirit to those who
ask Him?"' Luke 11:5-13

Jesus paints a picture of one man so desperate to meet the needs of a travelled and weary friend that he goes to great lengths, at a late hour and inconveniences a neighbour who has the needed supply. He refuses to give up until he gets what his friend needs.

Jesus uses this analogy to set the appropriate context for us, as disciples, asking for the Holy Spirit. Our determined motive is driven by the felt need to be able to meet the spiritual need of *others*.

This baptism with the Holy Spirit is modelled beautifully for us in the Book of Acts, by a post-Pentecost church now empowered to follow the same pattern of self-less ministry as Christ Himself.

In Acts chapter 3, on the way to the hour of prayer in the temple, Peter and John are met by the appeals of a lame beggar. Having themselves already spent the days leading up to Pentecost in prayer, asking, seeking and knocking, Peter and John now had a full shelf.

They told the beggar, *"Look at us!"* and, such was the manner in which they must have spoken to him, he did just that: *"... He gave them his attention, expecting to receive something from them."* (Acts 3:5)

He was right to expect to receive from them (- even if what they had wasn't quite what he was looking for!), as Peter said, *"I do not possess silver and gold, but what I do have I give to you: In the name of Jesus Christ the Nazarene - walk!"* (v. 6)

Our 21st century church should, likewise, be giving the world the same sense of expectation of receiving from us. And, as with Peter and John, they will sometimes end up with something more than they bargained for.

Thank God for humanitarian aid. I truly mean that, and I help lead a church that is committed to practical, compassionate help. But charity can be given by any human being, with or without Jesus Christ.

Pentecost opens up heaven's supernatural resources; empowering the gospel message; causing the kingdom of God to come in manifestation; resulting in remarkable church growth; creating a climate where people are talking about Jesus everywhere - for good or bad; shaking the institutions of society; and generally turning the world upside down!

Thank God for good deeds, but the world needs to see in the church the things only Jesus can do.

The longing in my heart to make disciples for Christ is left completely unsatisfied by the world around me saying, 'What a kind person Alistair is! What a good charity he leads!'

We do seek to give generously of our time and resources, but if we are only (at best) getting bigger and more popular, while our communities remain unchallenged and unchanged, then perhaps we need to rediscover why it is we are here?

If Jesus is not turning heads or capturing hearts in the market place, then perhaps it's time for us to return to the Upper Room to be refilled with the Holy Spirit.

Having skipped back in my thoughts to the lame beggar at the Jerusalem temple, let me leap forward to 1992 in the gorgeous Scottish Highland coastal village of Glenelg.

Peggy MacAskill, devastated by the tragic injury of her late-teenage son, Alan, who had fallen from a tree in the glen, had been travelling back and forth to Inverness to visit him in a comatose state that was now stretching into weeks, until something powerful happened.

Arriving in the ward one day, Peggy picked up a Bible that fell open at the story of Jesus raising up Jairus' daughter. As she turned to the body of her corpse-like son, all she saw was death, but at that moment she knew God would heal him.

When Peggy told the consultant what God was going to do, he could barely contain his frustration at a mother whose refusal to accept reality amounted to more of a hindrance than a help. The doctor was adamant: *"Your son has severe brain damage and there can be no recovery."*

Plans were already underway to transfer Alan to an English hospice for long-term care due to serious brain injury and, after all the consultant's efforts, Peggy was now complicating things. He turned briskly and exited the room in a way that spoke more loudly than words.

But that same evening, Peggy saw her son's finger move for the first time. Her faith began to grow. Having learned from a Christian nurse that there was a pastor named Samuel McKibben who prayed for the sick to be healed, she invited him to come and pray for Alan.

Arriving in the hospital, Samuel introduced himself to Peggy and then walked over to Alan's bedside. Understanding that Alan may be able to hear his words, Samuel began speaking, *"Alan, I'm sorry to hear about your accident, but I have good news for you because Jesus can ..."*

At that moment, Alan leapt to his feet and lunged towards Samuel's throat. Seeking to keep his attacker at bay, Samuel grabbed Alan's forearms as he raised his voice authoritatively and commanded, *"In the name of Jesus, come out of him! ... Be healed, in Jesus' name!"*

Alan fell back onto his bed, rolled over and returned to sleep.

Shortly afterwards, Samuel now gone, Peggy and her sister retired to the Raigmore Hospital refectory for an overdue bite to eat. They hadn't finished their meal before a doctor rushed into the cafeteria.

"A miracle has happened," he said, *"Your son is walking!"*

Several days later, Peggy took Alan back to the family home in Glenelg where he walked into the joyous embrace of a weeping father. Within a year, Alan had enrolled at a Christian Bible college in South Wales. A year after that, and out of this miracle, Glenelg Christian Fellowship began.

Nearly thirty years later, there is still a vibrant little church in that village which simply would not exist but for the power of the Spirit and two believers, Peggy and Samuel, whose larders were full.

When I last saw Peggy, a farmer's wife, ageing but still worshipping God with two generations of believing loved ones around her, I smilingly imagined a mother-hen surrounded by her chicks. When I think of her and my friend and mentor, Samuel, I see a Spirit-filled people, with purity of heart and power in their hands.

And then I think of Jesus, ascended to the Father yet still at work through His earthly body, all over the earth, just as He said He would be.

It is in the Person of the precious Holy Spirit, and Him alone, that all of Christ comes to be demonstrated in all the church.

8. THE BODY OF CHRIST

"... The church, which is His body, the fullness of Him who fills all in all."

Ephesians 1:22-23

C hristians can become so familiar with Bible language that we lose the wonder of what the words are actually saying, not just about Jesus but about us.

What must it have been like to be a new believer in a first century house meeting, soaking in the revelation of Paul for the first time? Imagine sitting into the night hours, riveted to a small Jewish man with piercing gaze, once described as hook-nosed, mono-browed and bandy-legged, yet with the face of an angel, as he spoke words like these ...

We are the body through which Jesus of Nazareth now speaks and acts. Wherever we go, by the Holy Spirit, He is filling everywhere with His presence. All that He is, He is in us. Where He is in heaven, so are we; where we are on earth, so is He ...

Had such teaching not been recorded in Paul's writings, and I were to write these words here for the first time, I should either be ridiculed as a fringe mystic or condemned as a heretic.

Just try, for a moment, to hear these words as if for the first time ... *"We are Christ's body, the fullness of Him who fills all in all."*

Yes, 'body' is a metaphor for our relationship to Christ rather than a concrete reality that makes us divine. No, we are not God. But 'body' is something more than metaphor - it speaks of Christ's identification with, and representation by, those in whom He actually lives by His Holy Spirit and considers to be inseparably His.

What's more, Paul declares that God's grand plan is for the whole cosmos to consider us inseparably His too, having *"raised us up with Him, and seated us with Him in the heavenly places in Christ Jesus, so that in the ages to come He might show the surpassing riches of His grace in kindness toward us in Christ Jesus."* (Ephesians 2:6-7)

The ascended Christ Himself was predestined to be observable in His people, the church. This will not be fully consummated until *"the ages to come,"* (Ephesians 2:7) but should also be demonstrated here and now, in this present age, by heaven's citizens, as the kingdom of God, the rule of Christ, is demonstrated through a Holy Spirit-filled church.

This is why Paul so prayed that the church would see with spiritual eyes what has already been accomplished by Christ. Only as we apprehend the wonder of what Christ has made us to be, *"created in righteousness and holiness of the truth"* (Ephesians 4:24), can we begin to grow up into a mature expression of that revelation.

I'm convinced the seeds of the doctrine of the church as Christ's body were rooted in Paul, or Saul, the moment he first met Jesus on the Damascus Road, when he was forced to identify Christ's followers with Christ Himself, by Jesus' own words: *"Saul, Saul, why are you persecuting Me?"* (Acts 9:4, emphasis mine)

As far as we know, Saul had never once met Jesus in the flesh. Yet when Saul participated in the martyrdom of Stephen, he became in reality embodied with the crowd that had cried out to Pilate, *"Crucify Him!"*

The Jesus who will one day judge the sheep and the goats with the words, *"What you did to the least of these, you did to **Me**,"* (Matthew 25:40, emphasis mine) is the One who considers the identity of His followers to be synonymous with His own.

When Paul embedded the idea that *"no one ever hated his own flesh"* in the example of Christ nourishing His church (Ephesians 5:28-29), as the model for husbands loving their wives, he was appealing to Christ's actual union with His church as a *sine quae non*, a fundamental, of the Christian faith: When Christ considers the church, He is thinking 'Me'.

As Saul discovered on the road to Damascus, where we are with Christ's people, is where we truly are with God.

So who are, and what is, this church?

In its fullness, the church is the universal assembly of every believer who will ever have lived, whose names have been written in heaven from before there was an earth.

But church should also be understood as the community that Jesus has been building since He ascended to heaven two millennia ago; the great company He spoke of when He told Peter, *"I shall be building my church."* (Matthew 16:18)

When Jesus left this world, it wasn't just to go ahead and prepare a place for us in heaven (John 14:2-3), but for Him on earth. The strategy, from His executive seat at the right hand of the Father, was to build a living temple, with us as 'living stones', by the agency of the Holy Spirit.

This temple is none of the things that true church has been sold short as: denominations, cathedrals and chapels, Sunday services and religious ceremonies.

Authentic church is built only by Jesus Christ - on the right foundation, using the right material, in the right way.

The Right Foundation

Genuine church has always been built on the same foundation: the revelation of who Jesus Christ is and what He has done.

> *"Simon Peter answered, '**You are the Christ**, the Son of the living God.' And Jesus said to him, 'Blessed are you, Simon Barjona, because flesh and blood did not **reveal this to you**, but My Father who is in heaven. I also say to you that you are Peter, and **upon this rock I will build My church**; and the gates of Hades will not overpower it.'"* Matthew 16:16-18 (Emphasis mine)

Much though many of us are endeared to, and identify with, Simon Peter, thankfully he is not the foundation upon which the church is built!

Church is not built on any apostle or prophet, but upon Christ and the revelation of Him. This is what apostles' and prophets' lives are built upon and their message flows out of. Anything else is of no use to the church, which can only be built on one foundation.

When Paul later wrote that *"no man can lay a foundation other than the one which is laid, which is Jesus Christ,"* (I Corinthians 3:11) he was not saying that apostles and prophets *are* the foundation, but that they *lay* it.

These ministries are foundational inasmuch as their message is the revelation upon which Christ builds His church. The apostle Paul spoke of *"my insight into the mystery of Christ, which in other generations was not made known to the sons of men, as it has now been revealed to His holy apostles and prophets in the Spirit."* (Ephesians 3:5)

The heart of apostles, gifted by Christ to lay the foundation which is Him, has always been to see the church solidly founded on revelation truth ...

> *"I pray that the God of our Lord Jesus Christ, the Father of glory, may give to you a spirit of wisdom and of revelation in the knowledge of Him. I pray that the eyes of your heart may be enlightened, so that you will know what is the hope of His calling, what are the riches of the glory of His inheritance in the saints, and what is the surpassing greatness of His power toward us who believe."* Ephesians 1:17-19

The revelation of *who* Christ is, and of the things that *are* in Him, is *"the foundation of the apostles and prophets"* (Ephesians 2:20) upon which He is building His true church. Nothing else is church.

It is because the knowledge of Christ, revealed fully in the New Testament, is the foundation upon which the church is built, that Paul wrote, *"... God has appointed in the church, **first** apostles, **second** prophets, **third** teachers ..."* (I Corinthians 12:28, emphasis mine)

Foundation first, then the building.

As Jesus pointed out in the Sermon on the Mount (Matthew 7:24-27), only a fool builds a house where the foundation is not solid.

And, if I may add to and update the metaphor in a way that reflects Ephesians chapter 4, you don't lay the foundation without the people who know how to pour concrete.

This is why the ascended Christ gives spiritual gifts to people, and then prepares and trains these servants in character and skill, in order that through them He might lay the foundation of a storm resistant church.

The 'poured concrete' is the revelation that is fully contained in Scripture; the *"wise master builders"* (I Corinthians 3:10) are the apostles, prophets and teachers who know how to lay that foundation.

How do we recognise the gifts and graces of the ascended Christ - *"apostles, prophets, evangelists, pastors and teachers"* (Ephesians 4:11) - at work?

We know them best by their effects, their fruit.

The Right Building

The evidence of an apostle in the house is a house that is apostolic.

The same is true for each of the five 'ascension gifts' of Ephesians chapter 4. They were not given to create an institutional, top heavy hierarchy with Christ up in heaven, us down here, and so called 'fivefold ministries' somewhere in between ... with apostles disappearing into the misty heights!

These ministries were not given to draw attention to themselves, but to equip, mobilise and mature the body. - the whole church, *"which is His body, the fullness of Him who fills all in all."* (Ephesians 1:23)

These ministries are spiritual leaders whose gift is the ability to cause the whole body to shine; to raise up a healthy church, every part engaged and harmoniously interacting, in a way that reveals an unmistakable, collective image of Jesus Himself.

It's not about the church any more than it's about its leaders: it's all about Jesus. This is the spirit that the church 'catches' off Christ-like leaders who, like Jesus, speak not of themselves but Him who sent them.

The church is not a 'club' that exists for the interests of its own leaders or members; it is the body, created to represent and express Him.

This is the proof that genuine apostles and pastors are in the house: the whole body starts to add up to Jesus.

> "And [Christ ascended] gave some as apostles, and some as prophets, and some as evangelists, and some as pastors and teachers, for the equipping of the saints for the work of service, to the building up of the body of Christ; until we all attain to the unity of the faith, and of the knowledge of the Son of God, to a mature man, to the measure of the stature which belongs to the fullness of Christ … from whom the whole body, being fitted and held together by what every joint supplies, according to the proper working of each individual part, causes the growth of the body for the building up of itself in love." Ephesians 4:11-13, 16

The Day of Pentecost was about so much more than ecstatic utterances: it was about the ascended Christ, Head over all things to the church, launching the mobilisation of His body on earth.

The *whole* church.

The venue for Pentecost was not Peter's personal prayer room. It all began in a gathering place where around 120 believers were *"all together in one place."* (Acts 2:1)

Of course, Peter was prepared and anointed to stand up and take the lead on that first day of great harvest. But what had commanded everyone's attention, gathered an eager audience and provoked the question - *"What does this mean?"* (Acts 2:12) - which provided the platform for the first sermon, was the astonishing sight of a Spirit-filled, emboldened community.

Not just old, but young also ... Not just men, women too - uninhibitedly preaching the mighty deeds of God.

God, by His Spirit, transgressed social hierarchies of respect, to make His purpose plain through His whole community: this is to reveal Jesus Christ, victorious over death and the grave, ascended to the right hand of the Father and releasing heaven on earth through the entirety of His Spirit-filled community.

This Spirit-filled Jewish church wasn't just blind to gender and age; it crossed ethnic boundaries too, speaking in the languages of all the Gentile nations represented, as the pilgrims gasped in astonishment, *"We hear them in our own tongues speaking of the mighty deeds of God."* (Acts 2:11).

People from these nations would soon be swept into the church by a gospel message that was about to flood the Gentile world, populating a spiritual collective predestined by God to reveal Jesus Christ to the entire cosmos; ultimately to display on earth and in heaven God's big picture for all creation.

It was this body, the church, that Paul celebrated in his letter to the Ephesians, a people of common citizenship who would amount to *"one new man"* (2:15), made up of Jews from near and Gentiles from afar.

The right building is the catholic (whole) church of Jesus Christ, the great company of every born again believer; a united body of Jew and Greek, male and female, slave and free; identified not by ethnicity, gender or social stratum, but heavenly citizenship; equipped, empowered and mobilised by the Holy Spirit to be the embodiment of Jesus Christ Himself; and authorised to represent His kingdom on earth.

No one part of Christ's body is sufficient to adequately reveal Jesus Christ - only the "mature man" of the all-inclusive body of Christ will accomplish that. This is what Jesus has been working on for 2,000 years; and it has been the longing of every disciple who has ever echoed the yearning of Paul:

> "... I, the prisoner of the Lord, implore you to walk in a manner worthy of the calling with which you have been called, with all humility and gentleness, with patience, showing tolerance for one another in love, being diligent to preserve the unity of the Spirit in the bond of peace. There is one body and one Spirit, just as also you were called in one hope of your calling; one Lord, one faith, one baptism, one God and Father of all who is over all and through all and in all." Ephesians 4:1-6

This has been the heart desire of every apostolic community in the history of Christianity. Why? Because it is the intercession of the Head of the body Himself ...

> "... That they may be one, just as We are one; I in them and You in Me, that they may be perfected in unity, so that the world may know that You sent Me ..." John 17:22-23

This great oneness is a work of Christ identified by Paul as *"the unity of the Spirit"* and is only accomplished by the Spirit's Person, presence and power in His church.

The Right Way

The right way is the way of the Spirit. Just as only a united church reveals Christ, so only a Spirit-filled church can be truly united.

Church only 'works' by the Holy Spirit. Contemporary professional models and traditional denominational structures may pretend to offer security - and there's much good to be found in both - but no organisation can compensate for the absence of the Holy Spirit's dynamic, manifest presence.

Only the Holy Spirit knows how to do real church.

On a visit to the magnificent basilica of St Peter in the Vatican City, I smiled at the irony of the Latin inscription circling the highest dome, quoting Jesus' declaration to Peter, which translates: "You are Peter and upon this rock I will build My church!" The irony was that the quotation was emblazoned in enormous lettering ... of gold! Imagine doing this with Peter, the one who declared in the power of the Holy Spirit, at the moment of his first recorded miracle, *"Silver and gold have I none ..."* (Acts 3:6)!

St Peter's basilica is for me the most impressive museum I have ever visited, but it is no more 'church' than our humble chunk of 1920s sandstone in Glasgow. Living church is not a monument but a movement, and its power to move and keep moving is only in the Holy Spirit.

Church is the *"dwelling of God in the Spirit,"* (Ephesians 2:22). The Holy Spirit has the know-how, power and nature to operate the church according to the will of its Head, Jesus Christ. Only by being filled with the Spirit can believers function in harmony with their Head and with the true body of fellow believers. Only in the fullness of the Holy Spirit do we begin to find our place in the big picture.

It should be no surprise to us that Ephesians, 'the epistle of the church', teaches so much about the work of the Holy Spirit in maturing the body of Christ to a full expression of Him.

The Spirit seals

> *"Having also believed, you were sealed in Him with the Holy Spirit of promise, who is given as a pledge of our inheritance, with a view to the redemption of God's own possession, to the praise of His glory."* 1:13-14

> *"Do not grieve the Holy Spirit of God, by whom you were sealed for the day of redemption."* 4:30

The Holy Spirit is the seal of those saved by grace through faith, set apart as Christ's genuine workmanship and guaranteed future glory.

The Spirit reveals

> *"... That the God of our Lord Jesus Christ, the Father of glory, may give to you a spirit of wisdom and of revelation in the knowledge of Him. I pray that the eyes of your heart may be enlightened."* 1:17-18

> *"... When you read you can understand my insight into the mystery of Christ, which in other generations was not made known to the sons of men, as it has now been revealed to His holy apostles and prophets in the Spirit."* 3:4-5

The same Holy Spirit who authored the Scriptures is the One who reveals their meaning to believers. God gave us our brains and desires us to worship Him with all our minds, but spiritual truth is revealed only by the enlightenment of the Holy Spirit, and our ability to understanding the Scriptures is determined more by our state of heart than the development of our intellect.

The Holy Spirit reveals not just *what* we need to know but *Whom* we must know and *why* we should know Him.

The Spirit gives access to God

> "... *Through [Christ] we both have our access in one Spirit to the Father.*" Ephesians 2:18

The Holy Spirit alone connects us to Jesus Christ. In the Holy Spirit we have assurance of son-ship and are empowered to emulate the same relationship with the Father that Christ came to model for us.

The Spirit makes us the dwelling place of God

> "... *In [Christ] you also are being built together into a dwelling of God in the Spirit.*" Ephesians 2:22

> "... *Being diligent to preserve the unity of the Spirit in the bond of peace. There is one body and one Spirit, just as also you were called in one hope of your calling.*" Ephesians 4:3-4

In English, the word 'you' serves as both singular and plural, but Paul uses the Greek *humeis* - 'you' plural - to describe the temple Jesus is building. It is the collective of Spirit-born believers, not the individual, that Paul here emphasises as the dwelling of God.

Only by the fullness of the Holy Spirit do we begin to marvel at, value and love the body of Christ as we ought; and only in that place of honouring His body do we begin to discover and flourish in our own place in it.

The Spirit is our source of inner strength

> *"... That He would grant you, according to the riches of*
> *His glory, to be strengthened with power through His*
> *Spirit in the inner man."* Ephesians 3:16

Paul wrote this awe-inspiring letter from a Roman prison. He was no stranger to jails, beatings, betrayals and hardships, and yet, even when encouragement could not be found in external circumstance, he was able to connect with unfathomable strength *within* - by the power of the Holy Spirit.

The Spirit is the bearer of Christ's gifts

> *"When He ascended on high, ... He gave gifts to men."*
> Ephesians 4:7

Jesus had said, *"Greater works than these he will do; because I go to the Father,"* (John 14:12) and His ascension to heaven is synonymous with His sending of the Holy Spirit and equipping of the church.

If Jesus commenced His own ministry with the words, *"The Spirit of the Lord is upon Me, because He has anointed Me to preach ...,"* (Luke 4:18) it follows that only by the anointing of the Holy Spirit will His delegated leaders be able to guide and equip His church in ministry.

The Spirit empowers a holy life

> *"... Do not get drunk with wine, for that is dissipation,*
> *but be filled with the Spirit, speaking to one another*
> *in psalms and hymns and spiritual songs, singing and*
> *making melody with your heart to the Lord."* Ephesians 5:18-19

These words should really be read in the context of the surrounding text: loving sacrifice, moral purity, controlled appetites, wholesome language, godly lifestyle, good testimony, wise decisions, spiritual vigilance and honourable relationships.

Unlike the Father and the Son, the *Holy* Spirit is the one member of the Trinity whose name includes a qualifying adjective: holy. Is there any more outstanding feature in the life of a Spirit-filled community than holiness?

The Holy Spirit alone is the one who delivers the church from contradictions and 'own goals', ensuring that there is no stumbling block in the life of the church to the gospel of Jesus Christ. The Spirit-filled church is the embodiment of integrity: a people whose message is fully *integrated* into its culture.

The Spirit handles the Scriptures and guides in prayer

> *"... The sword of the Spirit, which is the word of God. With all prayer and petition pray at all times in the Spirit."* Ephesians 6:17-18

Jesus was both filled and led by the Spirit into the wilderness, where He repeatedly batted into touch each temptation of Satan with the words, *"It is written ..."* It is by the enabling of the same Spirit that He equips His body to do the same.

And little wonder that when Jesus taught His disciples what we now call The Lord's Prayer, He immediately went on to add the instruction to ask, seek and knock for the Holy Spirit to be given (Luke 11:1-13). As Paul also wrote to the Romans, *"In the same way the Spirit also helps our weakness; for we do not know how to pray as we should, but the Spirit Himself intercedes for us with groanings too deep for words; and He who searches the hearts knows what the mind of the Spirit is, because He intercedes for the saints according to the will of God."* (Romans 8:26-27)

The way of the Spirit is the only way

It is one thing having the right foundation and the right building, but without the Spirit's immanent presence and power, the whole thing would be little more than philosophical theory and a hollow shell.

The church is the dwelling of God in the Spirit. The Holy Spirit is the Another-of-the-same as Jesus, the One who, out of the same union of the Trinity, ensures that the church is demonstrably the body of Christ.

With all this in mind, we appreciate afresh the urgency of Paul's command:

> *"Do not grieve the Holy Spirit of God ...!"* Ephesians 4:30

To exclude the Holy Spirit is quite simply to cease to be the body of Christ. Better to shut up shop and go home than be a hindrance to the cause of Christ by selling the world false goods.

Whatever is not the way of the Spirit is *in* the way of Christ, obscuring the big picture of God's plan of redemption.

When Jesus, on His departure, told His disciples to *"stay in the city until you are clothed with power from on high,"* (Lk. 24:49) He was implicitly saying, *Don't leave camp; don't even try to represent Me without being filled with the Holy Spirit!*

9. EVERY GIFT SUPPLIED

"...The same God who works all things in all persons."

I Corinthians 12:6

G od desires the fullness of Christ to be displayed through all of the church. Only the whole body is adequate for the task. The most gifted individual, even the most impressive movement, is much too small to come close to revealing the fullness of Christ.

The character and ministry demonstrated in the person of Jesus in the Gospels was continued after His ascension to heaven, by the Holy Spirit, through what we must understand as His body.

The earthly ministry of Jesus and the subsequent ministry of the church should not be seen as separate entities. The Scriptures narrate Jesus' ascension as a transition whereby He 'steps up' to 'next level' ministry, not just in heaven but also on earth. The punctuation mark and transition point between Christ's in-person ministry and its elevation and amplification to next level was the cross ...

"Truly, truly I say to you, unless a grain of wheat falls

into the earth and dies, it remains alone; but if it dies,
it bears much fruit." John 12:24

The single grain, which was Jesus, fell into the earth and died through the cross. But the reproductive power of His redeeming death produced a harvest of spiritual sons and daughters after Christ's own kind. This harvest would embody the multiplication of His ministry on earth, empowered by the Holy Spirit poured out upon His disciples after His ascension to the right hand of the Father, where He has ever since remained as *"head over all things to the church."*

The continued *earthly* ministry of the ascended Christ, by the agency of the Holy Spirit, is recorded in the Book of Acts and observable throughout church history.

Jesus Christ, as He said He would, is building His church today. And as His body grows spiritually, numerically and geographically, so the revelation and demonstration of who He is, is to be seen through the full supply of His gifts in a people whom the Holy Spirit continuously seeks to mature into His image.

This is the centre piece of God's cosmic plan, the big picture which every believer and every Christian community must grasp and invest ourselves in: *all of Christ in all the church to all creation.*

For us, experientially, it all starts in the local church. The same Holy Spirit who is at work universally is also at work in the small communities of believers where we find ourselves.

To us, Father, Son and Holy Spirit impart the ministries and graces necessary to continue the worldwide spread of God's Kingdom message and Christ's redeeming power on earth.

We will look at some of these gifts shortly, as Paul speaks to the Corinthians about *"the God who works all things in all persons."*

But first, a word about Corinth.

Corinth!

The Corinthians to which Paul wrote have been described as a dysfunctional church, yet lovers of truth should be grateful that their regrettable failings provided the opportunity for Paul to put on paper for us some of the most wonderful principles of how healthy church *should* function.

My first experiences of charismatic worship in the early 1980s forced me to wade through a gauntlet of opposition to the charismatic gifts that was particularly strong at that time. *"Beware of Corinth!"* I was warned, Corinth being a pseudonym for carnality and excess! *"... Keep clear of these charismatics!"* the alarm sounded, *"... Keep your feet on the ground and stay away from all that tongue-speaking and emotionalism ...!"*

But the warnings came too late! I had already begun discovering the charismatic phenomena in the New Testament. I was seeing them operating in a very special church I had just discovered, and I would soon start experiencing them in my own life.

Yes, spiritual stability is founded on truth rather than experience but the separation of truth and experience is neither realistic nor healthy. Biblical truth leads to and demands experience, and Jesus told His disciples to expect to be 'clothed' with the power of God.

Paul's response to the excesses of the Corinthians was not to bury their gifts under a wet blanket. On the contrary, he commenced his first letter by commending them for *"not lacking in any spiritual gift, as you eagerly await the revelation of our Lord Jesus Christ, who will also confirm you to the end, blameless in the day of our Lord Jesus Christ."* (I Corinthians 1:7-8)

Paul was in no way seeking to discourage charismatic phenomena, later adding, *"I thank God, I speak in tongues more than you all ..."* (I Corinthians 14:18). He was not advocating that everyone brings messages in tongues; he was simply pre-endorsing a wise maxim: *the solution to misuse in not disuse, but proper use.*

Paul did not advocate the abandonment of gifts of the Spirit any more than the abolition of the sacrament of Communion, simply because they had been guilty of abuse in that area also. Unfortunately, the excesses of Corinth were evident in pretty much everything they touched.

First Corinthians contains priceless principles that should not only promote the healthy operation of spiritual gifts and ministries, but also inspire the unity in diversity of a body matured in the love of God.

So how does the Spirit *"works all things in all persons"*?

'Effects' of the Spirit

> *"There are varieties of effects, but the same God who works all things in all persons. But to each one is given the manifestation of the Spirit for the common good. For to one is given the word of wisdom through the Spirit, and to another the word of knowledge according to the same Spirit; to another faith by the same Spirit, and to another gifts of healing by the one Spirit, and to another the effecting of miracles, and to another prophecy, and to another the distinguishing of spirits, to another various kinds of tongues, and to another the interpretation of tongues."* I Corinthians 12:6-10

One of the more under-emphasised purposes of the fullness of the Holy Spirit is that it is Christ's means of running the church. Christ builds His church by the Holy Spirit being in charge of us.

The kingdom of God, or the rule of Jesus, comes on earth by His people being filled with the Holy Spirit, the One who is the same in nature and purpose as the Father and the Son. *"**The kingdom of God**," as Paul wrote elsewhere to the Romans, "... **is** righteousness and peace and joy **in the Holy Spirit**."* (Romans 14:17, emphasis mine)

The kingdom of God is in the Holy Spirit. It is by our being filled with the Holy Spirit that Jesus is represented in us, revealing through us the same Father represented in Jesus.

When I pray, "Thy kingdom come!", implicit in that very prayer is the plea, "Fill me with the Holy Spirit!" There is no other way God's kingdom can come in my life, except through the personal, experiential fullness of the Holy Spirit.

This is as true for the collective as it is for the individual. Only a Spirit-filled church is able to glorify God by its testimony. This is why Paul concludes the above list of spiritual gifts by bringing us back to the One who is behind them:

> *"But one and the same Spirit works all these things, distributing to each one individually **just as He wills**."*
> I Corinthians 12:11 (Emphasis mine)

The gifts of the Spirit are expressions of the will of the Spirit of God. Hence these gifts are identified as *"effects"* of the Holy Spirit being present and at work.

The gifts of the Spirit have never been expressions of human personality or pet preference, but impartations of His initiative through whichever willing channel He chooses, *as* He wills, in a way that brings glory to the Source, God Himself.

As such, no Christian *has* these gifts - they are *His* in origin, operation and purpose. They are mutli-varied manifestations of *His* presence, through anyone He chooses, in any way He wishes, at whatever place or time He wishes to express Himself.

In contexts where I have observed these gifts operating, they have not always operated through those deemed the most naturally gifted or 'qualified'. The vessels will tend to be those humble enough to do what they believe they're being told, by the Spirit's prompting, sometimes (though not necessarily) with hands shaking and voice trembling.

Should He wish, He may decide to provide a gift of healing through someone we might usually expect to see teaching, or a prophetic utterance through a 'non-spiritual type' some would normally associate with practical or menial tasks.

There is no hiding from the Holy Spirit, no excuse to shelter behind when He stirs us to open our mouths or stand to our feet. I often think this is the real reason for the 'theological' objections of many who are, in truth, simply strong of will, fearful of and resistant to the idea of not being in charge.

And if some start getting used to exercising the same charismatic gifts repeatedly, the Spirit is at liberty to 'bring in others' as and when He wishes - just another reminder that He alone is the common denominator in Christ's body at work.

So Paul's use of the word 'effects' as distinct from, say, 'abilities', to describe these gifts, is an inference that they are means of God-expression, as distinct from self-expression (- which appeared to be something the Corinthians needed to learn).

These charismatic gifts, as effects, are once-off impartations of His grace and kindness, belonging to the Spirit who wills according to Christ, the Head of the church.

However, as time passes, in any Spirit-filled community where these effects are in operation, it will become evident that there are different motivations in different believers. In that sense, different believers do *have* certain gifts, but by stewardship rather than ownership.

The same Holy Spirit who is in charge of the gifts is also to be in charge of the disciples who are being equipped in their operation.

Motivational Gifts

As with all resources, natural or spiritual, it's good for us to *have* gifts ... just as long as the Holy Spirit *has us.* This is why we need to be continually filled with the Spirit.

Spirit-filled believers are to grow in their gifts as they grow in grace as disciples of Christ, human instruments of the Holy Spirit's will.

Gifts should not just be seen as things growing disciples *do*; they are outworkings of the part of Christ's body that we, as disciples, are growing up into ...

> *"Now you are Christ's body, and individually members of it. And God has appointed in the church, first apostles, second prophets, third teachers, then miracles, then gifts of healings, helps, administrations, various kinds of tongues. All are not apostles, are they? All are not prophets, are they? All are not teachers, are they? All are not workers of miracles, are they? All do not have gifts of healings, do they? All do not speak with tongues, do they? All do not interpret, do they? But earnestly desire the greater gifts ..."* I Corinthians 12:27-31

Underpinning the godly desire to have spiritual gifts is the realisation that they are a means by which the Holy Spirit desires to express the love of God through our servanthood.

This, the God-honouring love motive behind our use of spiritual gifts, is actually what the next chapter, the Love Passage (I Corinthians 13), so frequently de-contextualised for use in wedding ceremonies, is actually all about.

Where we are not maturing in the fruit of the Holy Spirit, the exercise of gifts, no matter how 'spiritual' they may appear to be, will have the same jarring effect on the observer as a clanging cymbal.

But the solution to the *abuse* of spiritual gifts as a means of self-expression is not *disuse*; rather, it is *proper* use by people motivated by love. The "better way" is not the "no gifts way", but the "gifts in love" way.

Spiritual gifts - *charismata* (Greek) - are outflows of the grace - *charis* (Greek) - of God in our lives, and we grow in them as we grow in grace.

Paul connects every gift to unique graces out of which they flow in a similar passage to the Romans ...

> *"Since we have gifts* [charismata] *that differ according to the grace* [charis] *given to us, each of us is to exercise them accordingly: if prophecy, according to the proportion of his faith; if service, in his serving; or he who teaches, in his teaching; or he who exhorts, in his exhortation; he who gives, with liberality; he who leads, with diligence; he who shows mercy, with cheerfulness."* Romans 12: 6-8

Out of the grace of faith flows the gift of prophecy. From the grace of liberality flows the gift of giving. From the grace of cheerfulness flows the gift of mercy. And so on.

Because the gifts are of the Spirit, they operate out of the measure of the Spirit's grace at work in our lives. This is where the Corinthians missed it - they went beyond the grace of God and used gifts as a means of self-elevation rather than God-expression.

To say that we only operate spiritual gifts out of the grace of God, is not to say that we cannot grow in these gifts. We are to grow in grace, and as we grow in grace we should expect our gifts, as outflows of grace, to develop and increase.

This lies at the very heart of Jesus' own teaching on faithful stewardship, when He reminded His disciples that *"He who is faithful in a very little thing is faithful also in much ..."* (Luke 16:10)

Gifts are growers of character

It has occasionally been raised as an objection to charismatic worship that Christians should focus on the growth of character rather than the exercise of gifts.

This becomes a false dichotomy when we begin to see gifts as tools for service and, therefore, a means of interaction with, and spiritual growth in, the body of Christ.

Christian service of any type is an accelerator of spiritual growth, and this is no less true than with spiritual gifts - we only need to consider the occasion for discipleship training that the Corinthians' use of spiritual gifts provided for the apostle Paul.

Since when were gifts, distributed by God Himself, in competition with the character of the One who gave them? Since when were gifts an alternative to, or in competition with, growing in grace?

If Christ gives us something, He will hold us to account for not just using it, but growing in it. And if I demonstrate the characteristic of faithfulness, He will entrust me with more.

Of course, there will be abuses of gifts, but there are abuses in everything ... how we use money, how we use our position, how we use the Scriptures, and so on. There is nothing we use that cannot be subject to abuse, no matter how good that thing is.

If I use the Scriptures for point-scoring unconstructive criticism today, that is no excuse to throw away the Bible tomorrow. So why would any Christian want to consign the gifts of the Spirit to the vaults of history because some have mishandled them?

Again, the solution to abuse is not disuse, but proper use.

God gives us gifts to develop us as loving servants. Servants need to have something to give. The motivation of the Spirit is always to put others ahead of ourselves and find joy in the blessing and lifting up of those who come after.

As we mature in our use of our gifts, we desire not just to bless others but, as spiritual parents, to help disciples grow in their gifts and become a greater means of blessing to others.

Some Christians get stunted in their spiritual growth at this point. They find it hard to live in a world where the blessing is not coming through themselves; where they are not, as it were, 'conducting the orchestra'. Making way for the gifts of others is a grace essential to the healthy development of our own gifts.

There can be a very fine line between growing in grace as servants, which is healthy, and deriving our sense of value from the things we do and how effectively we feel we are serving.

As Christians, our value is derived from the blood of Christ that was shed on the cross, never from how impressive we feel we are at serving. To serve Christ, or anyone else, in order to feel good about ourselves is deeply flawed and a recipe for the misuse of spiritual gifts.

We must grow in the grace of making room for the gifts of others. This may sometimes mean putting our gift to the side to enable the emergence of a gift in others. To fail to do this is to stay small and, if we are leaders, it is to keep our churches small too.

So, having considered spiritual gifts, firstly, as charismatic effects of the Holy Spirit, and secondly, as tools for service that we grow in by grace, we come to a third level of gifting: leadership ministry.

As we grow in our gifts, we are being prepared for a greater measure of trust again: equipping others, next generation disciples, in the development of their gifts.

Church Leadership gifts

Paul identifies five ministries imparted by the ascended Christ to equip the whole body for service ...

> *"And He gave some as apostles, some as prophets, some as evangelists, some as pastors and teachers, for the equipping of the saints for the work of ministry, for the building up of the body of Christ; until we all attain to the unity of the faith, and of the knowledge of the Son of God, to a mature man, to the measure of the stature which belongs to the fullness of Christ."* Ephesians 4:11-13

Apostles, prophets, evangelists, pastors and teachers were given to the church by Jesus to equip, build up, unify and mature the whole church to the point where we collectively embody Christ's life and ministry.

These five ministries amount to the fullness of Jesus' ministry on earth: The Apostle, sent by the Father to bring His kingdom on earth; the Prophet, revealing the will of God and the heart of man; the Evangelist, preaching the gospel of salvation and healing the sick; the Pastor and Teacher, gathering God's flock and nourishing them with the truth.

When Jesus ascended to the Father, He poured out all of these ministry giftings through the Holy Spirit to leaders who would, in turn, cultivate all these aspects of His ministry in the entire church.

The purpose in an apostle or evangelist today is to cultivate the expression of Christ the Apostle and Christ the Evangelist in the life of every believer.

If Christ dwells in a believer by His Spirit, and if Christ is an Apostle, then there is the spiritual DNA of an apostle within that believer. The 'apostle within' is the ambassador of Christ that is conscious of His Great Commission to leave no earthly boundary, literal or metaphorical, uncrossed by the Gospel of Christ and the claims of His kingdom, until He returns.

This does not make every believer an apostle; it makes every believer a part of the Apostle, Jesus Christ, who is to be revealed by the entirety of a mature, united church, His apostolic people. To stir up every believer, and to equip the church in its apostolic calling and potential, Jesus gifts and sends apostles to the church, as 'specialists' in this aspect of His ministry.

No one leader or local church has the 'full package' of Jesus' ministry, or anything remotely close to it, but when a breadth of gifting is in the house it ignites, mobilises and matures the church in the various graces that different leaders carry, as examples and igniters.

This is why – and I choose my words carefully – it can only be a ploy of Satan to banish certain gifts to the vaults of church history. The effect of this error, despite the best intentions of some who have ignorantly taught it, is to quench the Holy Spirit by stifling expressions of Jesus through His living body today.

We know when these five ascension ministries are in the church, not because we have a few spiritual 'super heroes' strutting our platforms, but because they raise up an empowered people, a fully engaged and healthily functioning body of believers who collectively make Jesus undeniable to the world around them. These ministries do not exist for themselves but to release the fullness of Christ through the whole body.

> "... The whole body, being fitted and held together by what every joint supplies, according to the proper working of each individual part, causes the growth of the body for the building up of itself in love." Ephesians 4:16

Unlike the once-off expressions of charismatic gifts in worship and the healthy operation of motivational gifts such as prophesy, teaching or practical helps, leadership ministries carry a level of authority and influence on the government and life of the church that requires the testing of time before they can be released. And even then, they must be subject to accountability, not just to Christ Himself, but to other leaders in Him.

In preparing for the recognition and release of these gifts, there is one stand-out hallmark repeatedly alluded to by the apostle Paul.

Faithfulness

What we may be unaware of as we skip from chapter to chapter through the Book of Acts, is that the period from the point of Saul of Tarsus' dramatic conversion until the point where he was sent out on his first apostolic circuit along with Barnabas was fourteen, maybe seventeen, years.

It was not until this time that he began reaching out to Gentile rulers, turning cities upside down, and writing all these epistles that have become foundational to the historic Christian faith.

Question: What was Paul doing during these years, before he was laid hands upon by the leaders at Antioch in Acts chapter 13, and sent out by the Holy Spirit for the commencement of his full blown apostolic ministry?

Answer: Being faithful.

Paul said so himself. The Greek word he used, translated 'faithful', was *pistos*, the word from which we derive 'piston'.

Paul was being piston-like, ever-dependable, year-in-year-out, fair weather and foul, preaching the same gospel revealed to him by Jesus, dependable with every task of service, regardless of the cost, not for recognition or reward, obeying each command with joyful gratitude, going where he was sent.

To put it in just a few of Paul's own words ...

> *"I thank Christ Jesus our Lord, who has strengthened me, because He considered me faithful, putting me into service."* I Timothy 1:12

> *"In this case, moreover, it is required of stewards that*

one be found trustworthy." I Corinthians 4:2

And then finally, in his parting epistle, Second Timothy, what does Paul urge of Timothy in selecting those who may be trusted to lead after they are both gone?

> *"The things which you have heard from me in the presence of many witnesses, entrust these to faithful people who will be able to teach others also."* II Timothy 2:2

Having been proven faithful, one whose word was good, who finished the things he started, reliable with the small, the mundane and the concerns of others than himself, he could now be trusted to go all the way to the executioner's block in Rome without damaging the Testimony.

It is a faithful church that reveals the Faithful and True, Jesus Christ Himself.

Thank God for the tools, the gifts and callings of Jesus, imparted by the Holy Spirit to His people, in order to reveal all of Christ through all the church.

Thank God that Jesus poured out the full panoply of His own gifts upon the church; if *He* needed these, then we far more!

And thank God for the Holy Spirit who not only imparts the abilities of Jesus, but also works into our lives the nature and character of the one who went all the way to the cross.

There were no works of Jesus in the Gospels that were not also displayed through the church in the Book of Acts, except one: the redemptive work of the cross itself.

And yet, even though only the blood of Christ is redemptive, it is a powerful truth that His redemptive act is never more visible to the world than when His people enter into what Paul referred to as *"the fellowship of His sufferings."* (Philippians 3:10)

There is absolutely nothing of Jesus, even the redeeming power of His death and resurrection, that is not to be made visible and known through message and testimony of His living expression on earth: the church, *"which is His body, the fullness of Him who fills all in all."* (Ephesians 1:23)

PART III: ALL CREATION

10. KOSMOS

*"For God so loved the world (Greek:
kosmos, created order), that
He gave His begotten Son, that
whoever believes in Him shall not
perish, but have eternal life."*

John 3:16

I 've occasionally heard well-intentioned preachers declare,
*'If you were the only sinner in all the world, Jesus would have
come and died for you.'*

Appealing though such an idea may be in a modern world where
the individual has become the centre of the universe, it is based
on a hypothetical impossibility.

Wherever the *if-you-were-the-only-one* imagination came from,
it is certainly not to be found in John chapter 3 verse 16. When
God gave His only begotten Son, it was the *kosmos* He was after!

God's great motivation in sending His Son was the redemption
of the entire created order, at the centre of which was mankind,
made in His own image and entrusted with Earth's stewardship,
but fallen in sin.

One of the first things we discover about God is that He doesn't 'do' individualism. As we have already seen (Chapter 2), God is a Trinity, an eternal communion of Three Persons - Father, Son and Holy Spirit - that has never existed outside of relationship.

Despite the suggestions of some, God didn't create us because He was in need of company, or because Heaven would somehow be relationally empty without us. The Trinity managed well for eternity before we came along.

When He created the cosmos, the great pantheon that John (1:3) simply calls *"all things"*, God designed a vast, harmoniously interacting order, the crowning jewel of which was mankind, created with a spiritual nature like His own.

In Genesis chapter 1, notice at the end of each day how God looked at His creation and *"saw that it was good."* It was evidently the subject of conversation going on within the Trinity, as they ultimately agreed:

> *"Let **Us** make man in **Our** image, according to **Our** likeness; and let **them** rule over the fish of the sea and over the birds of the sky and over the cattle and over all the earth, and over every creeping thing that creeps on the earth."* Genesis 1:26 (Emphases mine)

The work of the Trinity is completed at the end of the sixth day, with God considering His cosmos to be *"very good."*

Now, test your Bible knowledge!

Question: When was the first time in Scripture God declared something **not** to be good?

Answer: The very next chapter ...

> *"Then the Lord God said, '**It is not good for the man to
> be alone**; I will make him a helper suitable for him."*
> Genesis 2:18 (emphasis mine)

Why would God actually make a statement about it, now recorded in our Bibles, rather than simply quietly creating Eve and
moving on without pause, if He didn't want to emphasise the
completion of the creation of man in His own image as a plural-
ity (with the ability to multiply)?

Genesis 2:18 is obviously and justifiably a bedrock of the insti-
tution of marriage, but it also celebrates the essential nature of
community and inter-dependence that God wove into the DNA
of the human race.

Why would such a God ever wish me to visualise a scenario
where I were 'the only person in the world'? Why would God
ever want such an idea to be appealing to me, much less want to
appeal to such an idea in me?

The Me-only sentiment, I can only conclude, must trace itself to
the Fall. It belongs to a self-centred worldview that is possibly
the biggest hindrance to us beginning to see, much less collabor-
ate in, God's big picture and cosmic purpose.

Kosmos

Please do not be intimidated by the Greek word *kosmos* - it's all
over the New Testament! *Kosmos* has 188 appearances, more
than half of them in the writings of John, and most of these in
the Fourth Gospel.

John the Baptist introduces Jesus as *"the Lamb of God who takes
away the sin of the **kosmos**,"* (Jn. 1:29) the same *kosmos* that was
created through Jesus the Living Word (Jn. 1:10), who has now
come to purchase the redemption of that *kosmos*. (Jn. 3:16)

Again and again, John writes of Jesus and the *kosmos.* He even brings it into Jesus' prayer life (translated from Aramaic by John), with Jesus asking the Father, *"... May they be one, just as **We** are one ..."* - note that eternal relationship again! - *"... so that the [kosmos] may know that You sent Me ..."* (Jn. 17:22-23, emphasis mine)

But the *kosmos* has been corrupted by sin and has malfunctioned ever since our first parents ate the forbidden fruit. God loves the *kosmos* as He created it, but hates what has been done to it, having been estranged from Him through sin ... So, *"do not love the kosmos,"* John tells us, *"nor the things in the [kosmos]. If anyone loves the kosmos, the love of the Father is not in him. For all that is in the kosmos, the lust of the flesh and the lust of the eyes and the boastful pride of life, is not from the Father, but is from the kosmos."* (I Jn. 2:15-16)

But the corrupted *kosmos* is not forever! John reveals that it is destined for destruction, and that those who know Him will be delivered out of it ... *"The kosmos is passing away, and also its lusts; but the one who does the will of God lives forever."* (I Jn. 2:17)

The same Lamb of God who became the sacrifice for sin in John's Gospel becomes the reigning redeemer in John's Book of Revelation ... *"... There were loud voices in heaven, saying, 'The kingdom of the kosmos has become the kingdom of our Lord and of His Christ; and He will reign forever and ever.'"* (Rev. 11:15)

In the age to come, Jesus Himself will restore and reign over a replaced (not recycled) *kosmos* ... *"a new heaven and a new earth"* (Rev. 21:1), as God originally created and intended: something that works perfectly!

That restored order will be populated by a redeemed human race whose bodies, just like the planet, have been buried perishable but *"raised imperishable"* (I Cor. 15:50-53) in glorified bodies, the resurrected Christ Himself having been the *"first fruits"* and forerunner (I Cor. 15:20-22).

An Orderly, Harmonious Creation

Kosmos does not just speak of the vastness of the universe, the totality of all things; it speaks of working order.

God's original *kosmos* was a harmoniously interacting, perfectly functioning operation; an integrated, complementary system of diversity in unity, and unity in diversity.

Kosmos, interestingly, is used by the apostle Peter to describe a woman's clothing and style (- note the English word 'cosmetic') ... "*... Your kosmos must not be merely external - braiding the hair, and wearing gold jewellery, or putting on dresses; but let it be the hidden person of the heart, with the imperishable quality of a gentle and quiet spirit, which is precious in the sight of God ...*" (I Pet. 3:3-4)

God's original *kosmos* was a thing of beauty, poetry in motion. It worked harmoniously. As we have seen, God Himself *"saw that it was very good."*

Until the serpent entered the garden.

Broken Kosmos

Lucifer, banished from heaven for his mutinous attempt on the throne of God, came as a serpent and fed into Eve not just an appetite for forbidden fruit, but an ambition for personal supremacy ...

> "*... In the day you eat from [the tree of the knowledge of good and evil] your eyes will be opened, and **you will be like God** ...*" Genesis 3:5 (Emphasis mine)

Through sin, epitomised in the desire to take the place of God, the pristine perfection of the *kosmos* was corrupted. That's when everything started to go wrong, and the *kosmos* has paid with multiplied interest ever since.

If only Adam's sin could have been a 'Me-only' moment! But 'Me-only' doesn't happen in the *kosmos* that God created.

When man was corrupted by sin, everything he touched, directly or indirectly, became infected.

Disorder and dysfunction followed. Guilt clouded human conscience. Fear and insecurity invaded, with lying and deceit and every kind of sin imaginable.

Sin was, and remains, the mother of all viruses.

Man died spiritually the day he first sinned, separated and alienated from God.

Man cannot be at enmity with God without entering a state of conflict with his fellow man and, for that matter, the entire created order. Next, Adam's son was murdering his brother, and as soon as there were enough people to have a war, we started having wars.

Our stewardship of the planet, driven by greed and power-lust, brought destruction wherever we went, to the point where we are now polluting even our oceans and bulldozing our natural rainforests.

Many have pointed out that we are destroying the planet and killing our grandchildren, but still we cannot stop any more than the proverbial sinner unable to lift himself off the ground by his own proverbial boot laces.

This is the Fall. This is sin. This is Me-Myself-I.

Wherever we dethrone God, we build altars to self. We conquer the world and make the colonials wear our clothes and speak our languages. We race to the moon and plant a flag to display our superiority. And if we ever inhabit Mars, we'll take human pride, the footprint of the Fall, there too.

Like Lucifer, like Adam and Eve, like the builders of the Tower of Babel, we must sit in the seat of God and establish our dominance over the *kosmos*. God wanted us to run it for Him, but we wouldn't have it: we had to have it all for ourselves.

Oh, how depressing!

Thank God, the story didn't end there.

God loved the *kosmos* that He had created and sent His own Son, the fullness of all He is, to redeem the *kosmos* from what Satan and the mutinous sons of Adam had turned it into.

A Redeemed Kosmos

The Bible tells us that there will be a future age when Jesus Christ, having paid the price of the sin of the *kosmos* by His blood, will return to finally destroy and replace all the effects of the Fall. As we have seen, there will be a new *kosmos* ...

> *"Then I saw a new heaven and a new earth; for the first heaven and the first earth passed away, and there is no longer any sea. And I saw the holy city, new Jerusalem, coming down out of heaven from God, made ready as a bride adorned for her husband. And I heard a loud voice from the throne, saying, 'Behold, the tabernacle of God is among men, and He will dwell among them, and they shall be His people, and God Himself will be among them, and He will wipe away every tear from their eyes; and there will no longer be any death; there*

will no longer be any mourning, or crying, or pain; the first things have passed away.'" Revelation 21:1-4

When Paul describes Jesus as the last Adam, he declares the most wonderful truth in the history of mankind: the *kosmos*, including anything and everything that was corrupted through the sin of the first Adam, is now to be made subject to the influence of redemption.

Of course, being 'subject' to the influence of redemption is not the same as being redeemed. The Bible does not teach 'universalism'; the notion that everyone will go to Heaven and the planet will be restored to perfection, just because Jesus paid the price.

The blood of Christ was certainly valuable enough to pay for such a universal purchase. But Man, a free moral agent, can, does and will continue to reject His wonderful redemptive act. This rejection began when Jesus was here in Person ...

> *"He was in the kosmos, and the kosmos was made through Him, and the kosmos did not know Him. He came to His own, and those who were His own did not receive Him ..."* John 1:10-11

But, thank God, John continues ...

> *"... But as many as received Him, to them He gave the right to become children of God, even to those who believe in His name, who were born not of blood nor of the will of the flesh nor of the will of man, but of God."* John 1:12-13

Redemption is about destruction of evil and replacement with good, rather than the recycling of something corrupted at its core.

Redemption in Christ is by new birth. As it will be with the future heaven and earth, and the future of believers' resurrected bodies, it is not about an improved, or recycled, life but an exchanged life; the replacement of the believer's old with Christ's new; death and birth.

Redemption is not about 'the old me' doing my best to improve with God's help, but about the old me crucified, the birth of a new creation, and Christ living His life through me.

To truly 'join the church' is simply to be born of the Holy Spirit through faith in Christ, and thus become part of what the New Testament calls 'the body of Christ.' By being born again, we each become part of the body of Christ through which He, not self, is expressed.

Of course, just because Jesus has paid the price to redeem everything, doesn't means it's going to happen; in fact, the Bible says it will not happen. But for those who believe, it does.

Believers become part of the big picture of redemption: God's cosmic plan to make all of Himself known, through all of Christ, in all the church, to all creation.

The believer is not only saved from sin, but delivered out of a tiny, isolated bubble called 'Me' and into the grandest, most glorious story imaginable. The centre of my universe is no longer I but Christ, and I find life and fruitfulness in exactly the same way Jesus did on Earth: by living out of Communion with God, speaking only what we hear Him speak, and doing only what we see Him do.

As was the example of Christ's earthly ministry, so it continues to be in His heavenly ministry, demonstrated through His body, the church, in the *kosmos*. The redeemed now become His instruments of redemption. Jesus, through His earthly body, the church, continuing His ministry from 'upstairs', from the executive suite in heaven, from the right hand of the Father.

And wherever we go in the *kosmos*, everything we touch becomes subject to the influence of the Head over all things to the church, our influence a permanent and growing indicator of what will be, in the age that is to come.

The human race, the centre-piece of the *kosmos* created in the image of God, with the power to say yes or no, will continue to receive and, sadly, reject His redeeming power.

> *"... Go into all the [kosmos] and preach the gospel to all creation. He who has believed and has been baptised shall be saved; but he who has disbelieved shall be condemned. These signs will accompany those who have believed: in My name they will cast out demons, they will speak with new tongues; they will pick up serpents, and if they drink any deadly poison, it will not hurt them; they will lay hands on the sick, and they will recover."* Mark 16:15-18

Just as all mankind became subject to the Fall in Adam, there is no person on earth who is not now to receive the offer of redemption in Christ, through the message His church speaks and the Spirit-empowered life it lives.

Before the day when the King of creation Himself returns to usher in a New Heaven and a New Earth, Jesus has authorised His body, the church, to proclaim salvation through faith in Him.

Many will receive and many will reject our message, together with the accompanying signs that point to the Day when healing and deliverance will no longer be needed - who needs a 'Heaven' road sign in Heaven?!

Until that day, we not only preach the Gospel to mankind with signs following, but bring the influence of God's kingdom to the institutions of society and the entire created order.

Our very presence and behaviour are to declare Christ's 'added value' to absolutely everything we touch as the Creator's influence is reconnected to His creation. Unbelievers are able to bring this seasoning effect too, but only because Christ's influence has touched them too, whether they realise it or not.

Christian sociologists speak of 'redemption lift'. When souls are saved, they not only find personal salvation and bring the Gospel message to those they know; the elevating effects of their salvation shape those surrounding them and coming after them.

God's order is established in believers' lives and in their homes. Their children learn 'success behaviours' and achieve more in life. Where the Gospel impacts, culture changes, society's institutions are enriched, justice and equity are enhanced, economic productivity is increased, even the natural environment is stewarded in a way that honours its Creator.

Everything touched by the first Adam is to be touched by the second. Everything infected by sin is to be exposed to, and feel the effects of, the antidote of redemption through the shed blood of *"the Lamb of God who takes away the sin of the kosmos."* (Jn. 1:29)

Proverbs 14:34 described 'redemption lift' long, long before today's sociologists, with the words: *"Righteousness exalts a nation."* Actually, Paul taught the Romans (8:19) that the scope of redemption is far greater than even nation states: *"... The anxious longing of the creation waits eagerly for the revealing of the sons of God."*

The revelation of God's cosmic plan, *all of Christ in all the church*, is to extend to *all creation*, but its central concern is mankind. And its core mission is the redemption of men and women, the world over.

11. TO THE ENDS OF THE EARTH

*"I looked again. I saw a huge crowd,
too huge to count. Everyone was
there—all nations and tribes, all
races and languages ..."*

Revelation 7:9a; The Message

I have only once visited Israel. It went beyond my imaginations as I found myself transported in time at the shores of Galilee, the Jordan River, the sweeping Mount Carmel vista from the Galilean hills across Armageddon Plain all the way over to the 'Great Sea', not to mention sites too numerous to list in the Old City of Jerusalem. For a lover of the Scriptures it was an almost dizzying experience, from beginning to end. But there was one day-trip that rises above the rest in my memory: Joppa!

As we meandered through modern-day Jaffa to the traditional home of Simon the Tanner, perched above the Mediterranean, we happened upon an almost comical, balloon-like sculpting of Jonah's great fish, only 200 yards short of our destination.

My entire trip was worth it for this moment alone. An inner light bulb went on as I connected up two famous Bible stories for the very first time.

It dawned on me that the very place where Jonah had fled from God's command to preach to the Gentiles of Nineveh was the same geographical location where Peter succumbed to the call to preach the Gospel to the Gentiles of a Roman centurion's household.

The Gentile Pentecost

The significance of this locale was surely not lost on Peter. As a Galilean well out of his own northern comfort zone, he may have arrived in Joppa with a mind-set of discovery not that dissimilar to today's Holy Land pilgrims. Such out-of-context environments can sometimes be the fertile setting for fresh, bigger-than-me, outside-the-box perspective. It was to be a place of world-changing encounter for Peter, and perhaps the biggest game-changer in the Book of Acts.

According to Acts chapters 9 and 10, it was here, well off the beaten track, that Peter found himself at the epicentre of perhaps the most significant 'crossroads moment' in early Christianity. It was here that, under the direction and empowerment of the Holy Spirit, the faith of Abraham flew the nest of Jewish orthodoxy, and the spiritual foundation was finally completed for a truly worldwide movement.

As he descended from Simon the Tanner's rooftop overlooking the Great Sea, did Peter carry with him the vision of the prophet Habakkuk (2:14), his spiritual canvas filled by the glory of the Lord covering the peoples of the earth as the waters cover the sea?

Before we give Jonah too hard a time for having to hear the word of the Lord *"a second time"* before eventually obeying, it's worth noting that Peter's revelation required not two but three plays: just like Jonah, his first response was, *"By no means, Lord!"*

By the days of the first Christian disciples, the cultural chasm between Jew and Gentile was as great as ever, the religious taboos still enormous. Peter knew exactly what kind of response his revolutionary revelation would get from the church's Jewish leaders back in Jerusalem (- see Acts 11:1-3), never mind the scribes and Pharisees intent on gathering evidence for their religious-political courts.

What took place after Peter travelled from Joppa to Caesarea has been described as the 'Gentile Pentecost', when the Holy Spirit had the audacity to bypass Moses and the Law - not to mention interrupting Peter's sermon! (Acts 10:44) - in pouring out salvation upon Cornelius' household, with the same spiritual phenomena experienced in Acts chapter 2.

A Crimson Cord

Peter made that Spirit-led journey for the very moment that Jesus Himself had come to open His disciples' eyes to; for an episode that epitomised the calling to which God had raised up Abraham in the first place, the commission that was woven like a scarlet thread throughout the Old Testament. The parting words of the resurrected Jesus alluded to that same crimson cord:

> "... You will receive power when the Holy Spirit has come upon you; and you shall be My witnesses both in Jerusalem and in all Judea, **and Samaria, and as far as the remotest part of the earth.**" Acts 1:8 (Emphasis mine)

The aged Simeon had grasped the cord too, and was finally able to depart this world in peace, knowing not only that the great hope of Israel had finally arrived, but that Israel's eternal purpose to the nations would soon be back on track, now to be fully realigned through the child in his arms:

> *"Now, Lord, You are letting Your bond-servant depart in peace, according to Your word; for my eyes have seen Your salvation, which You have prepared **in the presence of all the peoples: a light for revelation for the Gentiles**, and the glory of Your people Israel."* Luke 2:29-32 (Emphasis mine)

What Habakkuk and the prophets had foreseen, Simeon actually touched in the infant Jesus, the One to be introduced to us by John the Baptist as *"the Lamb of God who takes away the sin of the world."* (John 1:29)

God's plan of redemption was always intended for the sons of Adam, never merely the sons of Abraham. Abraham, from the moment of his encounter, was raised up as God's conduit to the nations - he was to exist for them, not they for him. And all for the glory of God.

God had commissioned Adam to *"be fruitful and multiply, and fill the earth, and subdue it."* (Genesis 1:28) He later commissioned Noah to *"be fruitful and multiply, and fill the earth."* (Genesis 9:1) God's purpose was that His glory should be known throughout all His earth, by all mankind, the race created after His own image.

But we know what happened: sin entered. Yet God eventually found in Abram a man though whom His redemptive purpose could be extended to His fallen race. To Abram, God said:

> *"... I will make you into a great nation, and I will bless you, and make your name great; and **you shall be a blessing**; and I will bless those who bless you, and the one who curses you I will curse. And **in you all the families of the earth will be blessed**."* Genesis 12:2-3 (Em-

phasis mine)

In Abraham, we see the basic principle that God's people are blessed in order to *be* a blessing. The moment human blessing turns inward and becomes an end in itself, rather than a means to the end of blessing others, is the moment it ceases to serve the glory of the One who blessed. At that moment, God's blessing is corrupted.

So when Jesus came into the world, He came not only to provide redemption, but to raise up a body of people through whom His wonderful redemption would be made known to *"all the families of the earth."*

But very soon Jesus found Himself at loggerheads with Abraham's descendants. The corruption of God's blessing was epitomised in Jerusalem the day Jesus made a huge mission statement by turning everything upside-down in the temple ...

> *"And He entered the temple area and began to drive out those who were selling and buying on the temple grounds, and He overturned the tables of the money changers and the seats of those who were selling doves; and He would not allow anyone to carry merchandise through the temple grounds. And He began to teach and say to them, 'Is it not written: "My house will be called a house of prayer for all the nations"? But you have made it a den of robbers.'"* Mark 11:15-17

This would have happened in the Outer Court, also known as the Court of the Gentiles. This was the very place where the Gentiles should have been flooding in to worship God, but it had been selfishly owned by 'the blessed', and was now used to extract as much profit as possible for 'the blessed'.

The Jesus who turned over the tables was the same one who had just cursed the fig tree, a symbol of the fruitful people that Israel were called to be: a means of blessing to all peoples.

And so, before Jesus pours out the great Gift of the Holy Spirit at Pentecost, He makes it explicitly clear that this blessing is also the church's means of empowerment to be His witnesses to *"the ends of the earth"*.

Then on the day of outpouring, just in case anyone hasn't got the message yet, the Spirit supernaturally enables 'the blessed' to speak in the numerous languages of the Gentile nations represented at the feast. Pentecost was not conducted in Hebrew or Aramaic, but through an upward- therefore outward-looking people to the audience for which Pentecost was intended: the nations of the earth.

Now, in Acts chapter 2, the audience was composed of travellers from afar gathered for the feast, including not only dispersed Jews but also "proselytes", Gentiles converted to Judaism from the nations represented; hence, all the languages. But what happened in Acts chapter 10 was a radical departure again. This was the point where, once and for all, it was divinely demonstrated that Gentiles no longer had to come via Moses in order to discover Jesus and, through Him alone, receive the blessing of Abraham.

The Gentiles should no longer be considered unclean without having first embraced the customs of the Jews. No ceremonial initiations were any longer required, no Jewish rites, practices or eating habits to be observed, before receiving the gift of the Holy Spirit. Salvation was now clearly available by the grace of God through faith in Jesus Christ alone!

From this point on, the blessing of Abraham would explode indiscriminately up into Syria and Cilicia, around the Mediterranean Basin and into the most distant Gentile nations. By the early 2020s, the New Testament has been translated into well over 2,000 languages, covering over 90% of the 8 billion people alive today.

But Jesus Himself prophesied that before the end comes His gospel will be preached to every one of our more than 7,000 people groups still to be reached. And the crimson cord, from Genesis to Revelation, will ultimately lead us into all eternity. The aged John, transported to the throne of the Lamb on the Isle of Patmos, described the scene in heaven: "... *a huge crowd, too huge to count. Everyone was there - all nations and tribes, all races and languages.*" (Revelation 7:9, The Message)

An Apostolic People

Peter's coastal journey from Joppa to Caesarea was his ultimate *step-out-the-boat* moment as he left the confines of 'safe religion' and set foot upon the seas of the Gentiles. This time the apostle didn't sink.

As we drove back to Jerusalem from Jaffa that day, I began to reflect on Peter's noon-day housetop revelation as his third *follow-Me* moment, the commissioning that led to the complete unfolding of his call in Christ. Peter the evangelist had been called from the Sea of Galilee to become a fisher of men (Luke 5:10-11); Peter the pastor-teacher was called by the same waters three years later to tend and feed Christ's flock (John 21:15-19); and now Peter saw like a prophet (Acts 10:9-16) and was sent as an apostle (Acts 10:19-48), authorised to burst the cultural dam that withheld the blessing of Abraham from the peoples of the earth.

Like Moses' crossing of the Red Sea to the children of Israel, or Caesar's march across the Rubicon River to the Romans, Peter's 40-mile journey to Cornelius' house was to the church of Jesus Christ a game changer from which there would be no turning back; a watershed moment out of which, two millennia later, I, a

Gentile, writing largely to Gentiles, rejoice in the blessing of *our* father, Abraham. (Galatians 3:29)

Thank God for the grace to pastor, teach and preach the gospel, but throughout the history of Christianity the body of Christ has been led beyond the folds of the familiar by the prophetic voice and apostolic authority of boundary-breakers, boldly and sometimes dramatically taking the gospel to literal and metaphorical 'regions beyond.'

Where there is no apostolic impetus, the local church will not survive for long. Apostolic people are inspired and led by 'big picture' people; fathers, martyrs and refuse to stay 'inside the box'; William Tyndales, John Wesleys and Amy Carmichaels, who lift our vision to new horizons; humble yet fearless leaders of spiritual encounter who love and obey Jesus above all, unwilling to bow to any convention or constraint that stands between Him and the ends of the earth.

Apostolic leaders don't allow the church to get cosy. They lead from the front rather than driving from behind, courageously crossing frontiers, their lives challenging the church with the question, *When was the last time you did something for the first time?* They inspire local church, no matter how small, to see itself as hub rather than terminus, mission base not mission field, a life source rather than on life support.

It is an apostolic people that has not just survived, but migrated, adapted and multiplied with the same gospel for 2,000 years, most markedly in the most hostile of contexts. And it is an apostolic people that, by the grace of God and the incarnation of Christ in its ministry, will continue to do so, whatever the odds, until it finally reaches the ends of the earth.

Yes, there is still a way to go. As I write, 42.5% of the world's people groups are still unreached by the church, with 2.18 billion people who have virtually no exposure at all to the message of redemption in Jesus Christ. Set against that the statistic that well over 90% of the world's cross-cultural Christian missionaries are working entirely amongst nominally Christian people groups, and the fact that less than one penny in every pound of all Christian giving goes towards pioneer church planting among unreached peoples, and we are left with one undeniable conclusion: the body of Christ at large is not apostolic.

Frankly, little is more restrictive to the Great Commission of Jesus Christ than well-intentioned, but seriously misguided, Christians who consign the ministry apostles and prophets to the history vaults of the first century AD. If ever apostles and prophets needed to be released in the body of Christ, it is today, in the face of the enormous missionary challenge to which the whole church needs to be mobilised.

Such a church in its final days on earth will embody what it means to be an apostolic people: inherently outward-looking in vision, all-embracing in culture, inspired yet unconfined by the past, global in vision while ground-breaking at home; a people confident in Him whose they are, bigger than camps and small corners, bold in obedience, reckless in generosity.

If Jesus' assurance of Matthew 24:14 is to be fulfilled, that before the end comes this gospel will reach every people group on earth, then it is a distinctly apostolic people that will become more evident than ever in the final days of this age.

12. TO THE END OF THE AGE

"And one of the elders said to me, 'Stop weeping; behold, the Lion that is from the tribe of Judah, the Root of David, has overcome so as to be able to open the scroll and its seven seals.' And I saw between the throne ... and the elders a Lamb standing, as if slaughtered ..."

Revelation 5:5-6a

In the Bible narrative, the 'Last Days' is the age of the church, the entire Christian era. The so called 'end times' were announced by Peter as he quoted the prophet Joel on the Day of Pentecost. As Jesus Christ is yet to return in the same way as He departed (Acts 1:11), we are clearly in the same historical dispensation today. Therefore, the New Testament church is, as it has now been for two millennia, God's end-time people.

The Church: God's End-Time People

We are left to conclude that over the past two thousand years, Jesus Christ, as Head of the Church, has been engaged in the kind of things He told the disciples He would be doing after He left.

With His first followers deeply troubled and insecure at the prospect of His imminent departure, He comforted them with these words ...

> *"Do not let your heart be troubled; believe in God, believe also in Me. In My Father's house are many rooms; if that were not so, I would have told you, because I am going there to prepare a place for you. And if I go and prepare a place for you, I am coming again and will take you to Myself, so that where I am, there you also will be."* John 14:1-3

Note again, the Greek tense in which these words are written speaks of continuous, ongoing work rather than a momentary, once-off, completed task. The tense does not convey what grammarians would refer to as 'punctiliar action'. Jesus was saying, *"I am going to My Father's house **to be preparing** a place for you."* There is nothing in the text to suggest that Jesus is not still preparing heaven for the arrival of all His followers throughout history. This is just one heavenly, unseen work of Jesus in these last days.

Jesus' ascension, as we have seen, has not ended His earthly work, but has delegated it by the Holy Spirit, under His and the Father's 'remote control', from heaven. In that sense, He is still very active in this world through His new earthly body, the church.

At the same time as He has been preparing His disciples' eternal dwelling in heaven, He has also been building His own *"dwelling of God in the Spirit"* on earth. Note again the continuous tense in Jesus' promise ...

> *"And I also say to you that you are Peter, and upon*

this rock I will be building My church; and the gates of Hades will not be overpowering it." Matthew 16:18

This is the ongoing work that Paul also wrote of to the Ephesians ...

"... You also are being built together into a dwelling of God in the Spirit." Ephesians 2:22

Peter too wrote of the same temple ...

"... You also, as living stones, are being built up as a spiritual house for a holy priesthood, to offer up spiritual sacrifices acceptable to God through Jesus Christ." I Peter 2:5

Growth Through Adversity

A mark of the last days, in their entirety, is that the church, the ongoing handiwork of Jesus Christ Himself, continues to grow unstoppably on earth.

Yes, Jesus said there would be hardship and attack from without, not to mention turning away from within - why should it be any different from what we saw in the microcosm of His own three-year, earthly ministry?

If He suffered, so would His followers; if He must carry a martyr's cross en route to bodily resurrection and heavenly glory, so should they ...

"Then I heard a loud voice in heaven, saying, 'Now the salvation, and the power, and the kingdom of our God and the authority of His Christ have come, for the accuser of our brethren has been thrown down, he who

accuses them before our God day and night. And they overcame him because of the blood of the Lamb and because of the word of their testimony, and they did not love their life even when faced with death.'" Revelation 12:10-11

Jesus' own power-packed earthly ministry ended in the passion and glory of His crucifixion, resurrection and ascension to the Father, only to be followed by an outpouring of salvation on pilgrims gathered from many nations.

And then, the end of The Book reveals His church following the same path as its Master: world-shaking power met with great tribulation, bodily resurrection at Christ's return, and the worship of the victorious sacrificial Lamb, the First-Born from the dead who championed the way, by an innumerable host from every tribe and tongue ...

"After these things I looked, and behold, a great multitude which no one could count, from every nation and all tribes and peoples and tongues, standing before the throne and before the Lamb, clothed in white robes, and palm branches were in their hands; and they cry out with a loud voice, saying, 'Salvation to our God who sits on the throne, and to the Lamb.'" Revelation 7:9-10

Revelation is a wonderful book. What a pity that the only book in the Bible that actually says you're blessed if you read it also happens to be the book most Christians seem scared to read! It was written as a lifeline of hope to believers immersed in the late-first century persecution of Domitian (AD80s), and perhaps also of Nero (AD60s) before that.

Revelation is a triumph of Messianic symbolism. Have you ever wondered why the victorious Hero of this book is portrayed as a Lamb, the perfect biblical figure of sacrificial death?

The Lamb Triumphant

The image of a Lamb seated and worshipped on the Throne of Heaven doesn't require words, but a banner might read something like this: Heights of Glory after the horrors of Golgotha!

What better picture of hope in the face of tribulation than that of the crucified Lamb Himself to present to a chosen flock who, themselves, were now being plunged into an era of intense persecution? The cross that was their Master's would now be theirs too – but so would be His resurrection and glorification.

If Jesus had to face His own *'son of perdition'* (Judas) doing his worst during *His* last days on earth, should the church be shocked if we too have to face the son of perdition (Antichrist) doing his worst in *our* last days? Did Jesus not repeatedly tell His disciples to expect the same as He got when it came to tribulation? Judas unleashed the forces of wickedness on Jesus, but not without Jesus' explicit permission as He passed him the dipped morsel (John 13:26-27) with the words, *"What you do, do quickly."* The cross of suffering, as Jesus repeatedly tried to get across to His disciples, was not to be escaped or avoided; indeed, Jesus' response to Peter when he tried to resist the cross was, *"Get behind me, Satan!"* (Matthew 16:21-23)

What could possibly be more heinous than putting the pure and holy Son of God through the cruel, slow death of crucifixion? The same God who allowed it for His Son, as His passage to glory, is the God who will allow it for those of whom His Son said, *"If they persecuted Me, they will also persecute you."* (Jn. 15:20)

This alone makes sense of the undeserved suffering of every child of God who has ever lived.

Glory Through Suffering

The tribulation of the cross was the only route to the glorious resurrection and ascension which crowned the great triumph of Jesus' redemption act. Judas' fellow conspirators had little idea that they were actually carrying out a masterplan too great for their finite minds to comprehend. Paul simply called it the wisdom of God ...

> "... The wisdom which none of the rulers of this age has understood; for if they had understood it they would not have crucified the Lord of glory; but just as it is written, 'Things which eye has not seen and ear has not heard, and which have not entered the heart of man, all that God has prepared for those who love Him.'" I Corinthians 2:8-9

The cross was God's means of greater glory. This is what Jesus had tried to get across to His disciples, as He prepared them for the necessity of His own suffering and death:

> "Truly, truly, I say to you, unless a grain of wheat falls into the earth and dies, it remains alone; but if it dies, it bears much fruit. He who loves his life loses it, and he who hates his life in this world will keep it to life eternal. If anyone serves Me, he must follow Me; and where I am, there My servant will be also; if anyone serves Me, the Father will honour him." John 12:24-26

Like a single grain producing a harvest, so Jesus' death would produce not only His own wonderful resurrection but also, in that resurrection, the first-fruits of a great end-time multiplication through His church, to be commenced in Acts 2 at the Feast of First Fruits.

Note also how Jesus applies the principle of the death of the grain of wheat not just to His own imminent death, but also as a spiritual law or principle for those who come after Him. His disciples' future suffering would not be redemptive in the same sense as His - only the blood of the perfect Lamb of God could pay the price for sin - but it would be through their suffering that His death would continue to be powerfully revealed.

Christ's Cross Revealed Through Ours

Who could deny, for example, how the power of Christ's willing death was displayed as Stephen was crushed under a torrent of rocks, crying out just like his Mentor before him, *"Lord, do not hold this sin against them!"* (Acts 7:60) I should be amazed if something of Christ's cross didn't begin to make inroads into the heart of a certain young Saul of Tarsus, as he looked on that day.

It was the early church father, Tertullian, who said more than a century after the first disciples, *"The blood of the martyrs is the seed of the church."*

Jesus Himself had prepared His disciples for the launch of the church age, which was to be a dispensation of both power and persecution, with the words,

> *"... You will receive power when the Holy Spirit comes on you; and you will be my witnesses* [Greek, *martures*, also translated 'martyrs'] *in Jerusalem, and in all Judea and Samaria, and to the ends of the earth."*
> Acts 1:8

Prepared for Suffering

It is a false kindness to fail to *"strengthen"* and *"encourage"* the church as Paul and Barnabas did the disciples in Lystra, Iconium and Antioch, with this message: *"Through many tribulations we must enter the kingdom of God."* (Acts 14:22)

Days of enormous testing have fallen on untold numbers of precious Christian believers who have, throughout the 2,000-years-and-counting of these last days, paid the ultimate price in ways as horrific as anything we read of anywhere in the apocalyptic literature of Scripture.

But for those who are called upon to pay the price of ultimate identification with the Lamb, the outcome of their moment of affliction is to be an immeasurable reward for all eternity. Such was the hope that took first century believers through their darkest moments ...

> *"Women received back their dead by resurrection; and others were tortured, not accepting their release, so that they might obtain a better resurrection."* Hebrews 11:35

Rewarded for Suffering

Some will be delivered from death; but for those who are not, a *better* resurrection awaits!

Paul put it movingly and poetically to the believers in Corinth and Rome, the latter of which, according to historians, was where Paul would one day be executed himself ...

> *"For momentary, light affliction is producing for us an eternal weight of glory far beyond all comparison."* II Corinthians 4:17

> *"For I consider that the sufferings of this present time are not worthy to be compared with the glory that is to be revealed to us. For the anxious longing of the*

creation waits eagerly for the revealing of the sons of God." Romans 8:18-19

In the great unfolding of God's bigger picture, suffering precedes glory. Just as Christ's affliction and death gave way to glorious resurrection and ascension, so the trials of His end-time body, the church, will in the age to come give way to the revelation, through the bodily resurrected sons of God, of His glory to all creation.

Labour Pains

In Romans 8, Paul writes of creation creaking at the seams in a way he likens to labour pains of childbirth, as it longs for a glorious age that will follow the sufferings of a fallen world. Like Jesus on Resurrection Sunday, we too, after night is over, will appear in glory. On that day, Paul appears to envisage all creation celebrating. It will be the church's own 'Easter Sons Rise' moment, as Jesus Christ Himself, Head over all things to the church, illuminates the splendour of His *kosmos.*

But before the, what are these days to be like? What are these labour pains? Did Jesus not tell us Himself? ...

> *"And Jesus answered and said to them, 'See to it that no one misleads you. For many will come in My name, saying, "I am the Christ," and they will mislead many people. And you will be hearing of wars and rumours of wars. See that you are not alarmed, for those things must take place, but that is not yet the end. For nation will rise against nation, and kingdom against kingdom, and there will be famines and earthquakes in various places. But all these things are merely the beginning of birth pains.'"* Matthew 24:4-8

And in the midst of it all, how are God's Last Days people to respond to the harrowing hour of 'this present darkness'? Are we simply to grit our teeth and bear it all, to survive until we finally stumble over the line?

Peter answers that question rousingly ...

> *"In this you greatly rejoice, even though now for a little while, if necessary, you have been distressed by various trials, so that the proof of your faith, being more precious than gold which is perishable, even though tested by fire, may be found to result in praise and glory and honour at the revelation of Jesus Christ; and though you have not seen Him, you love Him, and though you do not see Him now, but believe in Him, you greatly rejoice with joy inexpressible and full of glory, obtaining as the outcome of your faith the salvation of your souls."* I Peter 1:6-9

Victory Over Adversity

On the occasions I have travelled in so called Less Developed Countries, I have been wonderfully inspired by the extent to which the default mode of ordinary Christians is frequently one of a significantly greater joy and spiritual vibrancy than that back home in the 'comfortable' West.

The church of Jesus Christ, against astonishing odds, is alive and growing 2,000 years down the road because it somehow finds wings in the storm. Hardships and difficulties become the air currents to greater heights for a living, Spirit-empowered body that thrives, rather than survives, amid batterings it might be expected to go down under.

With Jesus at the right hand of the Father, the first century church negotiated the pains of rejection in Jerusalem, Nero's persecutions from Rome, and the intensified assaults of Domitian, during which John, himself exiled to Patmos, painted for a suffering church our example of the victorious Lamb that was slain.

This picture of overcoming victory in the midst of tribulation is a major theme of the Book of Revelation, providing progression, harmony and unity to the redemption narrative of the entire Bible. Jesus Himself prepared us for it in the Gospels ...

> *"... In the world you have tribulation, but take courage; I have overcome the world."* John 16:33

Equipped With Power

Yet, at the same time as Jesus and the first disciples ran the gauntlet of religious and state-empowered opposition, they also walked in supernatural power. Jesus Himself spoke of the *"greater things"* His followers would do on Earth after His ascension.

It was during the fiery days of late first century persecution that John recalled again the words of Jesus, spoken in the lead-up to His own arrest and trial ...

> *"Truly, truly, I say to you, he who believes in Me, the works that I do, he will do also; and greater works than these he will do; because I go to the Father. Whatever you ask in My name, that will I do, so that the Father may be glorified in the Son. If you ask Me anything in My name, I will do it."* John 14:12-14

These greater works, the equippings of the Holy Spirit already considered (Section 2), are the signs of the Kingdom; a Kingdom that has coming, will come, and is coming now.

The kingdom of God *has* come

The Gospels couldn't be clearer that Jesus Christ's first coming brought the kingdom of God to earth.

But what *was* the kingdom that He brought? It was the spiritual king-ship, or rule, of God. The Kingdom, in this sense, is wherever God reigns, and it was manifested wherever Jesus, the Son of God, spoke and acted in the authority of the Father and of heaven.

Matthew wrote much about the Kingdom, beginning by telling us how Jesus' ministry began ...

> *"From that time Jesus began to preach and say, 'Repent, for the kingdom of heaven is at hand.'"* (Matthew 4:17)

John introduced Jesus the same way when he recalled ...

> *"Jesus responded and said to [Nicodemus], 'Truly, I say to you, unless someone is born again he cannot see the kingdom of God.'"* John 3:3

In Matthew chapter 8, the Roman centurion understood the authority of Christ's kingdom when he said,

> *"... For I also am a man under authority, with soldiers under me; and I say to this one, "Go!" and he goes, and to another, "Come!" and he comes, and to my slave, "Do this!" and he does it.' Now when Jesus heard this, He marvelled and said to those who were following, 'Truly I say to you, I have not found such great faith with anyone in Israel.'"* Matthew 8:9-10

Jesus' 'dominion' was not an earthly reign, or some kind of geopolitical liberation movement. This is where Jesus' opponents, and even some of His followers at times, got it wrong. Jesus' kingdom was not about physical conquest of the rulers and realms of Earth, nor a re-establishing of the halcyon days of King David's empire, governed from earthly Jerusalem; rather, it was the demonstration of a spiritual and moral realm that was in stark contrast to the systems of the broken *kosmos*, a sin-corrupted world, so frequently marked by greed, power-lust and oppression.

> *"... Jesus called them to Himself and said, 'You know that the rulers of the Gentiles lord it over them, and their great men exercise authority over them. It is not this way among you, but whoever wishes to become great among you shall be your servant, and whoever wishes to be first among you shall be your slave; just as the Son of Man did not come to be served, but to serve, and to give His life a ransom for many.'"* Matthew 20:25-28

From the outset of his Gospel, in chapters 5-7, Matthew presents us with what has been described as Jesus' 'Manifesto of the Kingdom', the Sermon on the Mount, which sets out how citizens of His kingdom are to live in this world. He gets immediately to the heart of just who are the candidates for God's kingdom:

> *"He opened His mouth and began to teach them, saying, 'Blessed are the poor in spirit, for theirs is the kingdom of heaven.'"* Matthew 5:2-3

The kingdom of God is, to this world, a topsy-turvy realm in which the weak are strong, the last are first, the small are great, the rulers serve, the dead live, the poor are rich, the givers receive, and on and on it goes.

Jesus Himself epitomised the nature of the citizens of His kingdom in serving and ultimately laying down His own life as God's sacrificial Lamb for the sins of the world. It is this Lamb who ultimately sits on the throne.

All that said, Matthew recorded from Jesus' lips a still-future time when He would return, not as a meek servant but a mighty ruler, calling the nations to account and to judgement ...

"But when the Son of Man comes in His glory, and all the angels with Him, then He will sit on His glorious throne. All the nations will be gathered before Him; and He will separate them from one another, as the shepherd separates the sheep from the goats; and He will put the sheep on His right, and the goats on the left ..." Matthew 25:31-33

But that Judgement Day would not come during Christ's first visit, much though many wanted it and some expected it. Neither has it come in the 2,000 years since His ascension, and wherever a misled church has sought to impose such a dominion ahead of its time, the result has been corruptive and corrosive.

It appears Jesus' disciples were still looking for that future kingdom shortly after His resurrection. As Jesus was preparing His disciples for the spiritual kingdom that had accompanied His earthly ministry, some were still hankering after the earthly regime of King David ...

"So when they had come together, they were asking Him, saying, 'Lord, is it at this time You are restoring the kingdom to Israel?'" Acts 1:6

Jesus immediately put them right by making it very clear the kingdom they were to be looking for was a transfer of what they had been observing in Him as they would boldly and authoritatively witness to Him, accompanied by demonstrations of the Spirit and of power:

> *"But He said to them, 'It is not for you to know periods of time or appointed times which the Father has set by His own authority; but **you will receive power when the Holy Spirit has come upon you; and you shall be My witnesses** both in Jerusalem and in all Judea, and Samaria, and as far as the remotest part of the earth.'"*
> Acts 1:7-8 (Emphasis mine)

As we shall later observe Paul pointing out to the Romans, the kingdom that had come with Christ and continued coming through the church from the Day of Pentecost onward, is not a physical or political dominion, but a place where God's people are living in the fullness of the Holy Spirit.

As we have seen (Chapter 7), this realm of the Holy Spirit is one of spiritual purity and power, and it is a realm that, as history has demonstrated, has often been most dramatically manifested and rapidly spread in the darkest of days and most hostile of environments.

But no matter how far this kingdom extends, it will not have the geopolitical and environmental dimensions of the kingdom that is yet to come. There is a full manifestation and glorious physical display of God's kingdom on earth that is reserved for Christ's second coming.

The kingdom of God *will* come

Only Jesus' glorious return, with a new Heaven and a new Earth will ultimately put all things right. It was that glorious day that offered the great hope that saw the first believers through the enormous traumas of the first century, in the New Testament prophetic writings, especially of John in Revelation ...

> *"Then I saw a new heaven and a new earth; for the first heaven and the first earth passed away, and there is no longer any sea. And I saw the holy city, new Jerusalem, coming down out of heaven from God, made ready as a bride adorned for her husband. And I heard a loud voice from the throne, saying, 'Behold, the tabernacle of God is among men, and He will dwell among them, and they shall be His people, and God Himself will be among them, He will wipe away every tear from their eyes; and there will no longer be any death; there will no longer be any mourning, or crying, or pain; the first things have passed away."* Revelation 21:1-5

What a wonderful day that will be! The Fall finally corrected. No more death or separation from anything that is good. Weeping and mourning, pain and suffering, poverty and want, sickness and disease ... all gone, never to return. All the blessings that, in this present age, have the power to corrupt, will never again turn our eyes or our hearts from the One who has blessed, as we and all creation are immersed in and infused by glorious, incorruptible perfection, both within and all around.

Then, in the final chapter of the Bible, we are met by what was intended at the very beginning, in a section headed in the New International Version as 'Eden Restored' ...

> *"And he showed me a river of the water of life, clear as crystal, coming from the throne of God and of the Lamb, in the middle of its street. On either side of the river was the tree of life, bearing twelve kinds of fruit, yielding its fruit every month; and the leaves of the tree were for the healing of the nations. There will no longer*

be any curse; and the throne of God and of the Lamb will be in it, and His bond-servants will serve Him; they will see His face, and His name will be on their foreheads. And there will no longer be any night; and they will not have need of the light of a lamp nor the light of the sun, because the Lord God will illuminate them; and they will reign forever and ever." Revelation 22:1-5

Do you see the huge difference between this and the Eden of Genesis? In this scene, the river and the tree of life find themselves in a city, and in a world populated by nations; the great inhabited world of original purpose, which God had told Adam to multiply into and fill; the design of God that will be ultimately unthwarted by the Fall; a re-created world enhanced by the light of the Lamb who would never have been there, but for the sin for which He was slain before the whole thing began.

Eternal, glorious bliss!

It was this big picture of our ultimate destiny that Paul had in mind when he spoke of *"Christ in you, the hope of glory,"* (Colossians 1:27), the future certainty to which our present faith is fastened as the anchor of our souls, sustaining us with joy and enabling us to shine as God's lights in the present darkness.

The Kingdom that *has* come spiritually through Jesus' first coming, *will* come in full-blown physical manifestation through His future return. And in these last days, the in-between time, the Kingdom *is* coming through the church.

The kingdom of God *is* coming

When Paul talks of our *"citizenship"* as being of heaven (Ph'p. 3:20), he is saying that we, the church, belong to another realm, with a culture and standard of righteousness that couldn't be further removed from the fallen world which we are passing through.

When Peter describes us as *"a peculiar people"* (I Pet. 2:9), he alludes to a heavenly kingdom, an age that is to come. We live, as a holy nation, in a foreign dominion, that is fallen in sin, as aliens, or strangers, passing through.

The kingdom we represent is, according to Paul, a kingdom of *"righteousness and peace and joy in the Holy Spirit"* (Romans 14:17). Although the church is not the same as the kingdom, it could be understood as the embassy of the kingdom on earth. A Spirit-filled local church is a place where any observer should be able to observe the culture and values of the kingdom of God. This is a kingdom that, as we have seen, will come one day in manifest physical glory; it came spiritually in Jesus Christ; and it is coming now through Christ's body, the church.

We are sent by Jesus into all the world to preach the gospel of His kingdom, living according to its standards - not this world's - and carrying its culture wherever we go. This should make God's people 'game changers' wherever they appear.

There has been disagreement over the years on the extent to which Christians can expect to bring the kingdom of God, before Christ Himself establishes it on earth in the age that is to come. Two extremes should be avoided.

On one extreme, 'Kingdom Now' teaching has argued that the church will so establish God's kingdom on earth that there is no longer any need for Christ to return - some have even got into the heretical idea that Christ does not actually need to come back physically as He will already be here in us. Not wishing to leave Jesus out, some of these have suggested that, having won the world, the church will hand it all over to Him, thus ushering in heaven on earth!

On the other extreme, 'Kingdom Then' teaching has maintained that the world is so beyond redemptive influence that it will continue to go from bad to worse until Christ comes. Backsliding will leave the church a pure but unproductive remnant, marked with such ever-diminishing returns that any sign of growth or influence in society should be viewed with suspicion as evidence of compromise.

Both of these are obviously imbalanced views!

Thank God for a church that, just as in the days of Paul and Silas, is able to *"turn the world upside down"* (Acts 17:6), not just saving souls and healing the sick, but affecting economies, influencing public life and shaping entire societies, embodying kingdom values of righteousness, love and justice. Is this not what Jesus Himself urged in His 'kingdom manifesto' (The Sermon on the Mount), with these words ...

> *"You are the salt of the earth; but if the salt has become tasteless, how can it be made salty again? It is no longer good for anything, except to be thrown out and trampled underfoot by people. You are the light of the world. A city set on a hill cannot be hidden; nor do people light a lamp and put it under a basket, but on the lampstand, and it gives light to all who are in the house. Your light must shine before people in such a way that they may see your good works, and glorify your Father who is in heaven."* Matthew 5:13-15

God's kingdom people, the church, are to bring the redemptive power of God to bear in the here and now. This world system may be a spiritual 'Babylon', but did God not instruct His ancient covenant people to impact their place of captivity with His blessing? Are the words of Jeremiah to his compatriots of Babylonian captivity not equally valid for God's people in every historical context of ungodliness and oppression? ...

> *"Seek the prosperity of the city where I have sent you*
> *into exile, and pray to the Lord in its behalf; for in its*
> *prosperity will be your prosperity."* Jeremiah 29:7

These captives were, to use Jesus' later words, to be salt and light. So are we, the church, His kingdom people. We will not ultimately 'save the planet', but we are to demonstrate what heaven is like while the present form remains and, in so doing, win that great multitude which no one can count, who will one day bow before the Lamb in the future kingdom that He alone will bring on His return.

Christ, through His church, until the end of this age, will continue to extend the gospel of salvation and of His kingdom, with signs following, bearing culturally transformative impact on every possible sphere of public life, from personal morality to how we steward the planet, to every tribe and tongue on earth, all in the power of the Holy Spirit.

Sin in the heart of man is the centre of the problem, but the circumference of the Fall's reach will be touched also, and no effect of sin, direct or indirect, in the entire cosmos is out of bounds to the redeeming power and influence of Christ's cross. Before this world burns up, a people from every tribe and tongue will be redeemed as the Lamb's reward.

The New Testament is very clear that, just as all our physical bodies will either perish or be replaced at Christ's return with glorified, incorruptible bodies (I Cor. 15:50-53), so also the entirety of the physical world will be destroyed and replaced by a New Heaven and a New Earth (II Pet. 3:10-13).

But until that day comes, Christ is continuing to raise up and mature His whole church, equipping us with what the writer to the Hebrews describes as *"powers of the age that is to come"* (Hebrews 6:5), supernatural tasters now of what will be natural then.

Sickness and disease will not be banished in this present age, but they will be in the next. In the meantime, the church, as heaven's ambassadors, have been equipped to minister healing and deliverance, samples and wares of the coming age, which we represent now. Healing and deliverance in this age are signposts to a time when there will no longer be any need of them.

Those who are miraculously healed will die of something else eventually. Even Lazarus didn't have eternal life on earth. Healing is a visual aid of a kingdom of righteousness where there is no sin and there will be no death; it is also a demonstration of compassion and kindness, revealing a God of love and confirming the gospel message.

Crucially, healing is a physical picture of the ultimate disease from which every human being absolutely must be healed: sin ...

> *"'But so that you may know that the Son of Man has authority on earth to forgive sins' - then He said to the paralysed man, 'Get up, pick up your stretcher and go home.'"* Matthew 9:6

May we, the church of Jesus Christ, bring the joy of salvation wherever we go, declaring to a sin-crippled world, *'In the name of Jesus, rise up and walk!'*, even if sometimes, like Peter and John, the bank account is empty and we have to reach into spiritual travel bags and declare, *"I do not have silver and gold, but what I do have I give to you."* (Acts 3:6)

All Summed up in Christ

It is my prayer that, as you have read this chapter, you have seen a fuller glimpse of what Paul describes as ...

> *"... the mystery of His will, according to His good pleasure which He set forth in Him, regarding His plan of the fullness of the times, to bring all things together in Christ, things in the heavens and things on the earth."* (Ephesians 1:9-10)

Whether we see it or not, if Scripture is true, God, in these last days, really is bringing everything together in Christ!

I dearly hope that, having reached the end of this book, you will have glimpsed something more of the wonder of what I can only describe as the big picture, God's plan for everything ...

All of Christ in All the Church to All Creation

EPILOGUE

I 've frequently marvelled at these words of the apostle Paul:

"For we are His workmanship, created in Christ Jesus for good works, which God prepared beforehand so that we would walk in them." (Ephesians 2:10)

God's macro plan is filled with a vast diversity of micro elements, each and every part, though indispensible, finding its place in the whole.

When God thought of me, long before I was ever born, He designed me as a microscopic part of His big picture, a tiny creation that He would one day incorporate into His eternal plan.

This is why, as soon as I find Jesus, I start to discover and grow into my place in His body, the church. And as I, an individual, start to discover my place in Christ's body, I add another pixel to the world's image of Jesus.

God designed me to fit perfectly into my right place in The Plan, planted somewhere in the vast array of all His people. What an amazing thought that my fulfilment in Christ begins by simply accepting what He has made me to be!

I love how Mother Teresa described herself: *'a little pencil in God's hand.'*

It is not *who* I am that is important so much as *Whose* I am.

I do not need to impress, simply to surrender to Jesus and rest in the One who delights to bring glory to Himself by doing extraordinary things with ordinary vessels.

It's a thing of beauty, poetry in motion, to see humble people unconsciously flourish with a fruitfulness and attractiveness that proves there has to be more to it than them.

So where do I discover my 'zone', this place that so glorifies God, my locus in the big picture?

The purpose of *The Big Picture* is not to lose the individual in a cosmic ocean, but to sketch a setting much bigger than all of us, in which each part contributes to a more glorious image of Jesus than ever.

This is what our world needs and our Jesus deserves.

But no one benefits more from the assembling of the big picture than the individual, each one bathed in a light far brighter than could ever be generated in isolation.

It's a place accessed only through the cross, and entered under the glow of *'no longer I, but Christ in Me.'*

The truth is, I will never discover my place in it all by looking inward. I won't even discover it by *looking* for it.

That special place begins with with the worship of Jesus Christ, grows clearer through following Him, and ends up giving glory to Him. The fuller I discover Him, the brighter the intended *me* will shine ... by accident.

In his endorsement of *The Big Picture*, Phelim Doherty drew analogy to a large map in a shopping mall. You see where everything is, but you're searching for the little red 'X' that says, "**YOU ARE HERE**".

I pray that, through reading this book, your image of Christ will not only be enlarged, but your little red 'X' will stand out even more boldly than before.

BOOKS BY THIS AUTHOR

40 Days: Treasures Of Darkness

40 Days: Treasures of Darkness was written during the first wave of the 2020 Corona virus pandemic and is built upon the biblical premise that good things start in hard places.

The order of dark-then-light, night-then-day, death-then-life is repeated from Genesis to Revelation and is epitomised in the Light of the world, Jesus Christ Himself, who entered a world "sitting in darkness."

40 Days: Treasures of Darkness is no morbid preoccupation with gloom. Rather, it is a message of certain hope for anyone struggling with the worst this world is able to serve.

Your lowest ebb, your darkest night, is the place where God is more than able to meet with you, pick you up and lead you into a new day.

Printed in Great Britain
by Amazon